TO Crystal Durham

Falling in Love with
Jesus

May God bless you
and all of your endeavors!!

Dr. Monique Vann, D.M.

Love always,

Dr. Monique

Falling in Love with Jesus:

Embracing the true power of God's love for my life

Dr. Monique Vann, D.M.

Dr. Monique Vann

Table of Contents

Dedication

This book is dedicated to my best friend Jesus Christ. Its dedicated to every person that has ever struggled with an eating disorder or perfectionism. Its dedicated to those who lost their lives in silence to their eating disorder. To my best friend Michelle aka Sparkle thank you so much for pushing me to win in life and to always have my back. I'm so thankful for our friendship that God has blessed us to have it means so much to me to have someone that knows and understands and that loves me no matter what. To Dr. Michele Brown thank you so much for pushing me to write and to enter book contests and to never give up but to always keep believing. I celebrate you woman of God. To my auntie Prophetess Judy Porter thank you so much for your constant support in my it means so much to me. To Chanel Martin and the amazing group Write with me, thank you so much helping me to birth this book in an accelerated manner wow 7 days has been the most challenging and healing book that I have ever written. Thank you so much for your dedication to helping authors to win in life. To Victor and

Deneen Marshall and the Glory Network family thank you so much for pushing me to become more and to become greater. To Dr. Robin and Christian Harfouche thank you so much for the impartation that you have placed into my life. To Lakisha Harfouche thank you so much for always praying for me and for encouraging me. To my mom Genise Rodgers, thank you for your prayers. To my all my siblings, friends and family thank you so much for all your support. To Tamara Huff thank you so much for all your support.

Dr. Monique Vann

Introduction

In our most broken places in life we sometimes fall prey to believing that there are limitations to God's love for our lives and we end up believing this lie for so long that it then becomes real to us and it becomes so real to us that we carry it over in our hearts for years believing that it is true and it ends up blocking us in the process. That has been me for over 30 years I have been blocking love and not receiving it because I thought that I could control the pattern of love and how it existed and how it was intended for my life. Little did I know that I was harming myself more than I was helping myself. Being a student at International Miracle Institute changed my life. In two years, I was able to gain the impartation for my life that I needed to keep me and to help me to grow and develop in my relationship with God.

The next encounter in my life happened recently on July 14, 2019 I had an encounter with God at church on Sunday at Journey Church in Raleigh the worship team was singing a song by Hill Song called you loved me as you found me and I began to immediately break out in tears. For so long I had been searching for love. I had been searching for others to complete me. I had been searching for that perfect moment in my life to just happen. I was expecting a change in my life and when it finally happened, I knew that my life was never going to be the same. Where I had thought that I had to prove my love for God all this year and to prove my love to others that I was seeking a validity of love that did not need to be found. God has already loved me as he found me just as I was, he embraced me with more of his great love to help me to evolve and to become the woman of God that he had created me to be in life.

I want to welcome you to my process of love, my story of how God's great love came to love me just as I was and to make me whole and new again for his glory. In this book you too will come to embrace the power of God's love for your life in such a way that it will change you forever. May you know the power of God's love for you is so much greater than you can ever imagine or hope in. May you know and discover the beautiful love for your life that God has intended for you to walk in it and to embrace.

This is not just any story but its one that you will never forget. My prayer that God will breathe life into you as you read each page and that you will grow more in your love life with God after reading. Welcome to my journey of falling in love with Jesus. May your life now be forever changed as well through the power of his great love for you.

Chapter One

Love Found Me at my lowest point

For so long I have thought I that I had to be perfect to be accepted and loved and accepted by others. I spent so many years of my life trying to please others and to gain their approval for my life and their acceptance because I never thought that what I was giving or contributing was enough. I had carried this in my thoughts for years and it has impaired me so much so that it has caused my relationships in life to become affected. The perfectionist side of my life started at a young age. I grew up seeking the approval of my mother and my father. I sometimes overachieved at the sake of gaining approval that I felt was the validation that I needed in my life. Everyone that met me enjoyed my company and enjoyed having me around and I enjoyed this as well but at times it was simply not enough to be loved and accepted by others, I felt in my heart that there was more.

I was struggling with acceptance. I was struggling with how to love others. I struggled with perfectionism. I also struggled with the fear of man. This sort of control in my life had positioned me to not fully receive the love for my life that God had truly intended. I noticed that I was creating at times self-sabotage on my life. I always thought that I had to be perfect for others to really love me. My dating relationships never lasted long because of this concept in my mind. Early in my teenage years and in my twenties, I had struggled with bulimia. Bulimia or Bulimia Nervosa is an eating disorder that is characterized as being, "an emotional disorder involving distortion of body image and an obsessive desire to lose weight, in which bouts of extreme overeating are followed by depression and self-induced vomiting, purging, or fasting.

an eating disorder in which a large quantity of food is consumed in a short period of time, often followed by feelings of guilt or shame." At sixteen years old, I started eating food and then throwing it up. I would go out to eat with friends and then go hide in the bathroom feeling guilty about what I had eaten and not wanting to gain weight from what I had eaten. A lot of people don't believe that eating

disorders can affect women of color, but it affected me. I spent

several years of my life eating a lot of food and then making myself

throw up because I felt like it was the only control that I had in my

life was the control of my body. Even though I was destroying my

body and silently killing myself inside it was my way of coping

through the hard times that were happening in my life. I ran track all

four years of high school and I didn't get to enjoy my teenage years

as much as I could have because I had allowed the enemy to cause

me to believe that my size mattered that much and that my image

was not good enough. I thought I had to be a perfect model.

Sadly, no matter how small I had gotten it was never small

enough. This was a mental illness that was starting to take control

over my life. I was constantly worried about my appearance and

being perfect. I had started to pull back from hanging out with

friends and going to track practice when I was in high school. I was

involved in the choir at school, the Future Business Leaders of

America, and I ran track and worked at Taco Bell.

I started exercising and eating alone in order to gain the

figure and size that I thought that I had to be at to be loved. It took years of counseling and self-help groups to recover from the pain that had developed in my life from eating disorders. I had finished college at Oral Roberts University, and I was working on my doctorate degree at the time at Colorado Technical University and I started attending a church called Transformation Church. They had a session called the Encounter weekend that I attended and when I attended, I surrendered to God. I place my perfectionism, my eating disorders, my abuse, my approval addiction, and my fear of man on the altar. True freedom came in my life that day. Each day of my life after that was not easy but I had to learn how to walk out my deliverance and accept the freedom in my life that God had given to me and to help others to get their freedom before it's too late. Eating disorders are very serious and some people end of dying from them. I am blessed today that I did not die and that I am a survivor but my heart goes out to others that the pain of being loved and accepted and having control took them out before they had the strength to get the help that they needed.

Prior to my deliverance I learned that suppressing hurt would only deepen the issues even the more. According to Psychology today, "What a child does is make an unconscious or semi-conscious decision about what he or she needs to do to prevent

this—whatever the "this" is, be it abandonment, pain, fear, or loss of

control—from happening again." In other words, there were things

that I was traumatically holding inside of me that was causing me to

feel the way that I was feeling at the time and I did not even realize

this. This can happen without us even being aware. I have seen this

happen to people in my life that would snap or yell or become

angry. I realized that their anger was being triggered by something

that had affected them early on in life that they had not taken the

time to get healed or delivered from. That is why it is ever so

important to not rush into relationships without first dealing with

the deep issues inside of our hearts. It does not go away overnight it

has to be dealt with and handled properly for complete healing and

deliverance to take place. Some of the trauma that has been faced

may also take a saved man or woman of God in deliverance

ministry laying hands on us and casting the devil out of us.

Until the issues have been dealt with it will continue to

linger on for years causing trouble in our lives. I have seen this

happen during the holidays that heated arguments would transpire

out of pain and not knowing how to properly communicate on the things that had happened in the past that it had come to carry over into the present. All of this could have been resolved early on had it been recognized or spotted earlier in our lives. Some people are fortunate enough to get to the root of the issue early on and some are not. This was the case for me. I had not fully gotten to the root of my eating disorders and what had initially caused me to reach towards finding control in my life from the trauma that I had experienced in my past. A lot of times things were not stable, and my family and I ended up moving from place to place. We lived in a shelter and sometimes we lived with other people.

This pattern of going from place to place caused instability to formulate into my life. I found myself living from place to place and never feeling settled. I felt like there was somewhere I had to move to in order to feel right inside. I have been homeless five times. This is not normal, and it is not something to even brag about. It hurts that I allowed myself to become homeless or to even get to the place of living in my car and living out of hotels. There was something that I was running from inside of myself that I had not dealt with. I had to learn how to become stable and to not run away from the issues that were happening in my life.

Falling in Love with Jesus

Being homeless was very hard and painful and there were days that I would go and take a shower in Planet Fitness and sleep in my car and scrape up change in order to have something to eat. I would have to call and ask friends for help at the time and desperately pray that they would help. This is when I had to have a divine intervention in my life and want to change. I prayed and asked God to help settle my life and help me to stop running but to face whatever it was on the inside of me that I was going through.

I knew that I needed to learn how to love myself again and to forgive myself. I often allowed pride to keep me locked away from asking from the help that I needed to gain my true freedom and start experiencing the love of God completely in my life. I had to learn how to love myself again even if it meant starting off step by step to get there and finding the stability in my life was the first step in getting there. I had to learn how to budget, save, and not live above my means.

There were so many days that I beat myself up mentally rehearsing in my mind how I could have changed a situation or what I could have done better. Sadly, there was nothing that was ever good or enough or better because in my mind it had to be perfect in order to be better. The word perfect is defined as being, "having all the required or desirable elements, qualities, or characteristics; as good as it is possible to be; absolute or complete; make (something) completely free from faults or defects, or as close to such a condition as possible." Perfectionism was blocking the love in my life that I needed to embrace. Whenever anything was not perfect or met my expectations it forced me to shut down inside and not appreciate what it was that was being delivered to me.

My love walk with God is one that I have come to value, accept and to appreciate. One of the reasons for this is that God's love has been the keeping power that has helped me to overcome so many obstacles and changes in my life. I literally have spent days at times sitting and writing in my journal on the awesomeness of Jesus. For so long I have looked for that perfect book or that perfect song to help me to get what I needed from God. I have even searched and failed in marriage because my heart of love was not in the right place at the time. The truth is that in order to really love anyone I had to first come to the knowledge and acceptance of loving myself in all my flaws and imperfections. I have dealt with insecurities in the past that have caused me to reevaluate why I loved myself one day and then why I would at the same time despise myself this made no sense to me.

I had to sit down and find my purpose and move forward in the love that God had designed for my life for so long. My love was not predicated on the performance or mastery of others, it was not implied on how much love I planned to give out per day, nor was it exemplified in my actions daily. The secret to falling in love with Jesus is to truly become real with myself and with my emotions and see myself in the mirror for who truly am and then to flow in that. Love takes time to develop and to grow and it is not always easy to accept or to receive love because of what we may have experienced in our past or in our child hoods.

I grew up in a home that was filled with love but at the same time I was also empty and void because I was in single parent home without a father figure. I had to learn how to love and accept myself and then how to love others. No matter how hard I worked on loving and accepting myself it has been a hard barrier to overcome and it has been one of the hardest things to really face in my life. I often push people away that love me too hard because I have not come to terms with how to accept love. Love should be one of the easiest things for me to accept but instead it has been one of the hardest for me to embrace.

The next thing that I must learn how to do is to accept God's love for my life. In accepting his love, I then know that I can work harder at accepting myself more and embracing the woman of God that he has called me to become. It has been an upward battle for me to daily embrace this love walks, and it has meant so much to me to be able to master it and develop my relationship with Christ more through learning the power of forgiveness. When Jesus died on the cross for us, he knew the pain that he had to face beforehand. He knew the beatings that would come, the pain, the agony, the lies from others and the betrayal but even still despite all of that he still chose to love us and to die for us as an ultimate display of love. How greater than is my love for others and my love for my walk with God. I have found that in living for God it has been very challenging.

My love walk with God sets the tone for my love walk with others. In my stance of living and operating in this earth it is imperative that I emulate the love of Christ in my actions and not just in my words. As believers it is so easy at times to feel obligated in terms of our love with others and we forget the power that is defined through God's love for us. We must take the time to hear and obey all that God is speaking to us in this season and that way that we do that is through our walk with him.

Learning the power of God's love is extraordinary and we can fall in love all over again when we have taken the time to embrace and accept his love for us in our lives. The hardest part for me is accepting the love of the father and it should not be the hardest but I have allowed myself to be at this place in my life that I feel like I do not deserve God's love or that I am not worthy of his love for me. His love is for me and he has demonstrated his love for me in the ultimate sacrifice. Loving God is the best decisions that anyone can make in life because it is through his love that changes are made it is through his love that deliverance takes place, it is through his love that that healing takes place, it is through his love that true love happens in our lives. Falling in love with God has been the best thing that has happened to me because I have allowed God's love to overshadow me and to embrace my broken areas in my life.

His love has covered me so greatly that I have become changed through the power of God. His love has changed me in such a way that I have fallen in love with God. As a Christian and a believer, it is so easy to get lukewarm and stagnant, but God is so wonderful that our love should always grow stronger for God and we should always look to love him more and more each day. God's love supersedes our love in that he ensures us of how great his love is for us. There is nothing that we can do to separate his love from. I was in church this past Sunday and the power of God hit ne so strongly during worship. I knew then that my love for God had grown deeper than I can ever imagine.

As I grow and develop more and more in this season. I am looking forward to experiencing an even greater magnitude of God's love in my life. His love for me has looked past everything in the past that I have ever done and sometimes we may take those things for granted but God's love for us overlooks it all and it's just as if you have never committed a sin. When God has justified us it renews us, cleanses us and redeems us for a greater work for his Glory. I am excited about the newfound love that I have in Jesus and how he has changed my life. The greatest thing about my love walk now is that I do not plan to turn back and neither am I looking back because his love is just that powerful and just that wonderful to me. I look forward to seeking God and spending time with God because of his love for me.

I look forward to being changed and developed because I know that in that change, I am then becoming better. I am becoming renewed. I am becoming a new reflection of Jesus in all that I do and say in my life. My love walk cannot be duplicated because it truly is my walk with the father that is transforming me for a greater work and purpose. My desire is that my walk with the Lord comes to be one that is forever impacted by the greatness of our God. I want my love walk to cause others to want to have a love walk with the father.

The way to do that is to live my life in such a way that it pleases and brings honor to God. In this season it feels like God has done an open-heart surgery in me. It has been a process that has been mentally and physically draining to endure but God has endowed me through his healing and virtue. Sometimes we over analyze our past and what we have been through and we forget that God holds the final say in everything. We all have a past, but God has designed it to be solely that a past it is not designed to be our future but simply a testimony into our destiny in Christ. In Romans 13:8 it states that, "Owe no man anything, but to love one another: for he that loveth another hath fulfilled the law."

That is the beauty of it all that love has found me just as I am and has now helped me to overcome and to experience what real compassion is and how it is to be carried out in my life. I am on an endless journey of love and in that journey, I have included no baggage, but I have included a heart of expectation of the love of my father Jesus Christ. When I write to him, I call him Daddy God for he truly is my father, my lord, my savior, my everything. I know now that the love that has found me has helped me to heal in so many areas in my life and to push harder to help others to receive their healing in life as well. That is what love does it heals. That is what God's love does ultimately for us it heals. His love waits for you until you are open to receive it. There is nothing more beautiful than receiving the true love of Jesus.

When I began to fully embrace the love of Jesus for my life, perfectionism, eating disorders, approval addiction, fear of man, and insecurity was not able to hold me hostage anymore in my thought life. God's love looked beyond the pain and saw what I truly needed in my life which was love. The only approval that I needed to accept was the approval from God. I had given people too much power and control over my life and I had to separate from the negative and toxic relationships that were causing me to want to go back and starve myself again to feel like I had some sense of control in my life. God does not want us to harm ourselves to feel love and accepted neither does he wants us feeling that we are undeserving of his love for us. He loves unconditionally and we must learn that God's love is not like the love of family, friends, co-workers, or our team. His love supersedes beyond that because he has agape love for us which is the ultimate level of love that we could possibly receive.

Chapter Two

My Love Walk in Jesus

My love walk in Christ has been one that has been a journey that I indeed to stay on and never deter from because it is just that powerful of a journey. Walking my love walk in Jesus means more to me than anything that I could ever imagine. My love walk is simply that it is a walk of faith that has helped me to stretch in my life with Christ and have insatiable hunger for more of God's presence and God's love. God is starting something in new and afresh in me this season and he is using this time in my life as an opportunity to use my life as a testimony of his goodness and to help to change the lives of others.

In Ephesians 5:1-7 it says, "Therefore be imitators of God as dear children. [2] And walk in love, as Christ also has loved us and given Himself for us, an offering and a sacrifice to God for a sweet-smelling aroma. But fornication and all uncleanness or covetousness, let it not even be named among you, as is fitting for saints; [4] neither filthiness, nor foolish talking, nor coarse jesting, which are not fitting, but rather giving of thanks.

I must learn and understand what my love walk in Christ means to myself, to others and then to God. This will help me to better understand the problems that I have faced in life with love. It has always been with my relationships with men that I have found it the hardest to appreciate and value the love that they are trying to give me. I have often pushed it away and not acknowledged it because of my own selfishness, hurt, pain and lack of understanding.

I have fell in and out of love so many times and it has been for good reasons and some for bad reasons. I have not come to terms with why this has taken place in my life. One of the things that I want to work on changing in my life is the way that I see love and how to be a true imitator of God through his love for others. My love walk has had painful areas in it that are too painful at times to even discuss or to talk about. Becoming aware of God's love for me has helped me to want to share with others on how to love more and to gain healing through loving others through the love of Christ. We never know the power and the impact that the words I love you have on people but it truly does make an impact on people in a powerful way in that l love brings healing when we are able to forgive ourselves and to forgive others. When we come to terms of what our love for others resembles and how it is most pertinent to our walk with God and the image of how he sees and not how others see us.

Our love walk is worth the impact and change that we are going to bring to others through our change in our lives. When we think about a love walk it resembles moving, go forward in motion and not backwards and it also involves going up another level each time we walk like climbing stairs. Our love supersedes that when we allow God to take us to that true place of love and freedom in him. We begin to grow in our walk when we come to terms with how the love walk is to be carried out. I must look back at my life sometimes and just thank God that he has truly helped me to make it this far with his love and with his peace. His love has held me when I have been in my darkest place. Sometimes I have had to cry alone from the shame of things that have happened to me in my past that I could not talk to anyone about. God has loved me even through my shame and pain.

He has loved me when I did not have the strength or the energy to love myself. I have joy and peace in knowing that his love is building a bridge of hope for me and helping me to really see the power of how the love walk should be carried out and how each step is ever so important. I have learned how to take it simply one day at time and to not rush what God has for my life. Sometimes it's so easy to want to rush and to sprint and not take a slow walk or even a brisk walk to where God wants us to be that is where we have to step in and know that it is through the slow intimate walk that we have with God that we are fully able to embrace what he is saying and to embrace his true love for us. We can't get to it when we are in a rush and trying to hurry the process that God has for and not to not take time to breathe in and out what God is truly doing for us in his love for us. We have to know that there is something big that is going to evolve from the situation and we have to accept that even though it is painful what we are going through in our lives that taking it one step at a time and trusting God is the best resource that we can truly rely on.

His love for us carries us through every dark and painful place and positions us to grown more and to want to change because of the time frame that he has allotted not in the fast run ahead of us but in the slow walk that he has designed for our lives Sometimes the walk may seem extended and it may seem fast while we are going through our tests and trials but God helps us to hold on and to rely on him for strength even when we do not fill like we have the strength to keep going. I have had to do that numerous times because of what has happened in my life. It's okay to fall backwards knowing that there is a greater walk ahead of us that is going to keep us from wandering in this season.

Falling forward is what we want to essentially accomplish and reach in our lives. God honors our love and our gratitude to him, and he wants us to rely on him and to trust him. The only way to do this is through knowing the power of his love for us and how his love changes us and makes us new. His love for us is so mighty and powerful. God's love is here to transform us. When we learn how to walk with God and how to trust God and how to embrace his love for us, we can have a smooth steady walk with him. His love for us rolls over ever situation that we are faced with and it helps us to know that even in the pain and the struggles of life that he is here with us and that he is never going to leave us. He is going to love us more that we love ourselves because he just that powerful and his heart as our father is to love us, stretch us and to help us to grow more in our love walk with him. We can't get there are on our own. As babies in the faith and in the gospel as believers we must learn how to stand on our own two feet, and it takes crawling before we learn how to walk.

We must walk through some painful memories. We must walk past the painful people that have hurt us and still love them. We must love the unlovable why because it's our duty as believers and children of God to love God and to trust him. He waits patiently for us as we go through our challenges and as learn how to walk towards him more than our phones and social media. It is so easy to get caught up in what's happening that we miss what God trying to do in us. That is when we must keep going and to keep believing that he is able to do exceedingly and abundantly above all that we ask or think according to the power within in.

That same power of love is operating in us and making us whole and complete in him. He wants us to be renewed and restored and when we learn to let go and to truly trust God, we can then embrace the full power of his love for us. But it requires slowing down for a moment to truly embrace the father's love for us. In this love walk you may experience so many things that happen in your life but know that God has the final say and his love is victorious and he is going to see you through the moments of pain that you are going through he is going to see you through every place of failure in your love that you have encountered and he going to help you to face your fears and to replace it with more of his love in this season.

God's love is so powerful it goes beyond our finite thinking and it protects us, saves us, delivers us and keeps us from evil. The power of God's love brings us to a place where we must examine ourselves and come face to face with our issues so that we can

have a greater walk in Christ. Love grows deeper when we

exercise the power of it through walking it out God's way. When

we truly fall in love with Jesus there is a complete change and

transformation in our lives that takes place. In 1st Corinthians it

states that, "Though I speak with the tongues of men and of angels,

but have not love, I have become sounding brass or a clanging

cymbal. And though I have the gift of prophecy, and understand all

mysteries and all knowledge, and though I have all faith, so that I

could remove mountains, but have not love, I am nothing. And

though I bestow all my goods to feed the poor, and though I give

my body to be burned, but have not love, it profits me nothing.

Love covers us and keeps us when we least expect it because the

power of God's love is here to shield us from all manner of evil

and to help to propel into our destinies.

There is no greater love than the love of our father he called us

to greatness, and he called to do exploits for his glory. We will get

there through the power of his love for us. There is nothing too big

or too hard for God that will stop him from loving us. The more we pull away from God the closer that he pulls back into us to celebrate us and to welcome us back home. There are so many things in life that we face and encounter but when we are able to encounter the true love of the father and to see clearly how his love for us is so much greater than we can ever imagine it will never lose its power.

When we hold on to God's love and connect more to his power and his greatness that he has for us we can then find how true connection in his love through the close-knit bond that we have created. I have fallen more in love in writing this book than I can imagine. He has opened my eyes to want to love him even more because of he has never stopped loving me in all of my failures and in all of my past that I have done and I have even been a backslider and have turned my life away from God and chosen alternate lifestyles but he has waited there for me with open arms waiting to embrace me and welcome me back home when I have ran away from his great love for me.

The more that I have sought after God the more that I have wanted to experience more of his love for me and more of his presence regularly. We become so distracted at times with our lives and things that are going on that we forget to properly love and acknowledge Jesus. He is there waiting on and never leaving our side because we mean that much to him and he wants to care for us in all our mishaps and mistakes and show us the true power of redemption through his love.

I once imagined what it was like to really love and it was not till, I became married and later separated waiting on divorce that I understood the power of love and how love for a spouse is so much different than the love of our father Jesus. His love for us expands us in such a way that we are deepened to want to experience more of his great love because it is a love that is interestingly one that never ends. That is one thing that I loved because in marriage we can abandon our partners and we can say the wrong things and hurt each other and then work on solving it later but God's love is instant and he is ready to forgive and forget right away.

When we truly fall in love with God it brings us to such a place of fulfillment that we are not looking for anyone to complete us but God. When we acknowledge that our completeness does not come from others but that it comes through our love for God, we can then experience the power of his love and the magnitude of knowing that his love is real. The worlds love for us is not like the love of Jesus it is a cut throat world that we live in doggy dog every man for himself but we have to learn to walk forward in knowing that God's love for us does not have not any of those characteristics and that his love for us is stronger than we can ever imagine. On this new journey of love, I am no longer for ways to please others but when I please God, he helps me please others in my walk with him.

In Matthew 5:44 it says that, "But I say to you, love your enemies, bless those who curse you, do good to those who hate you, and pray for those who spitefully use you and persecute you," Ephesians 5:2 says that, "And walk in love, as Christ also has loved us and given Himself for us, an offering and a sacrifice to God for a sweet-smelling aroma." 1 John 4;7 says that, Beloved, let us love one another, for love is of God; and everyone who loves is born of God and knows God.

In my love walk with God I have found the following

scriptures to be most helpful and positional in my love for Christ.

When I became a believer in the faith, I was not aware of the

opposition form others that would come from it and I had to learn

how to lean and pull on God's love and the Holy Spirit for

comfort. In knowing and understanding God's love for my life and

for the walk that I was living it required the understanding of how love operates and functions and to understand this I had to understand how God's love operated and functioned specifically for my life at the time. I knew in gaining this understanding that it would better help me to walk more effectively as a believer.

1 John 3:16

"By this we know love, because He laid down His life for us. And we also ought to lay down *our* lives for the brethren."

1 John 4:7

"Beloved, let us love one another, for love is of God; and everyone who loves is born of God and knows God."

1 John 4:10

"In this is love, not that we loved God, but that He loved us and sent His Son *to be* the propitiation for our sins."

1 John 4:16

"And we have known and believed the love that God has for us. God is love, and he who abides in love abides in God, and God in him."

2 Timothy 1:7

"For God has not given us a spirit of fear, but of power and of love and of a sound mind."

Chapter Three

Fighting For my life

Often this word is a cliché to hear when people say that they are fighting for their life, but this has been my story for this season that I am literally fighting for my life. I am fighting to be all that God has called me to be and more. I have been fighting a fight that has been more of an inward battle. I have been fighting with my emotions and processing what is happening to me and going on. I feel like I need to fight more than ever before to be the woman of God that he has called to me to be. I am fighting to more kingdom minded and more kingdom focused than I ever have been before. The challenge to evolve into the purpose that God has called me into has been hard. In Romans 8:28, "And we know that all things work together for the good to those who love God and to those who have been called according to his purpose.

My purpose involves fighting this battle to reclaim my name and to reclaim the relationship with God that I have longed to get back to the place where I once was in God without distractions. I am fighting for my life in a way that I have never fought before. I am fighting for my life to live in God to produce the fruit that he called to me to have. The fight for my life has been so strong and I need to reach more and seek God more than I ever have before because he has called me to be a prophetic voice to the nations. I am fighting to reclaim the vision and purpose for my life in this season. Since I was a little girl and even in my adulthood.

I have had to fight to win the battle and I must fight harder to reach the point in my life that God is asking me to reach. When I move myself out of the way and allow God to move that is when things can shift and then things can really change in my life. God is stretching me more than I can ever imagine growing and to help others to grow and to keep fighting hard no matter what is happening and taking place. To keep going no matter what the situation looks like in front of me. I know that there is a purpose aligned to my destiny and that God has me on a process that is one that not the same as others. I can't react the way that I used to because there is so much more inside of me that God wants to deliver out of me to reach my true potential in Christ. I must keep pushing and moving further in God to embrace what he has for my life and to not stop in the process but keep moving, breathing, and reaching for all that he has in my life and more.

There is such a cry of desperation for me in this season that is pushing me to want more and to reach for more of God because it is through his love that I will find my healing it is through his love that I will be restored it is through his love that I will have my breakthrough in Christ and the power of his love is going to help me to stand on to not give up. The power of his love is going to help me to grow and to develop and to overcome the challenges that are before me and to escape what the enemy thought he was going to destroy me with. There has been so much warfare going on and there have been so many challenges that I have encountered over the past few weeks.

I thank you Lord that I can lean and depend on you to keep going and to keep pressing forward. I am trusting God to help mend my broken heart in this season from the pain that I have experienced from past relationships in my life. I can't even say that it was the individual that wronged me but what I can say is that God has helped me to capture what it means to fight hard for my life, testimony and my story. It's all for God's glory and not for my own. I must keep fighting because I know that my deliverance is going to help to bring someone else out and to rescue them from their situation. There is such a great beauty in knowing that God loves us even when we are in the battle and we are fighting to keep our heads above the water. That is when God steps in and lets us know that he's got this and that we are not in this battle alone. The warfare is painful and its stretching me because there is a greater work that God wants to do in my life. There is a transformation that he wants to bring through me and it can only be birthed out through the spirit. There has been a dramatic change in my life and my heart aches, and I want the pain to leave but it keeps lingering. I know that I am going through a process and that you have something powerful that you are going to do in me. So much has been going on in my life in the past months and it has been unbearable at times but my desire to grow in God has kept me on the melting pot of change and it has kept me on the potter's wheel of deliverance.

The pain that I feel right now is agonizing but I know that in writing my healing process has already begun and that there is nothing that can hold me back from God's love. I have allowed people to come in my life steal my time and to try to invade the purpose on my life but I know that I have to keep moving and keep going because there is a will and a fight inside of me to keep going to keep pushing and to keep seeking the face of God in spite of the challenges that I am facing in my life. There is no good thing that God will uphold from those who walk upright towards him.

I know that every time that I write a new book that the devil is going to try to do everything that he can to stop the word from going forth. It is the job of the enemy to plot and to scheme and to try to destroy us but when we are in Christ the word of God says in Isaiah 54:17, " No weapon that has been formed against us shall be able to prosper." I'm going to keep fighting for life because I know that this battle that I am facing right now is not my own but that it belongs to God. He is testing me now to get me to the place that I need to be in him, and the purification process is never easy once we have been tainted God. God then must cleanse us and to deliver us. We must keep moving forward even when it feels like we are being pulled in the opposite direction. The Holy Spirit is telling me that many of you that is reading this book today is being faced with an challenge that seems insurmountable and you feel like there is no hope for your situation and the fight that you once had is gone. Keep on fighting hard to get back to the place in God that you need to be.

There is a divine call on your life that is pertinent to your process. You must keep moving even when there is no confidence in you go forward and to trust God that he is going to help you through it all. The more we press in the more we keep moving towards the promise of God and not the promise of ourselves we will then be the true warriors for God that he has positioned us to be in this earth. We fight for the ones that we love and God's love for us is the same way he is fighting to help us to keep moving forward in the things of him and God is fighting to protect us and to shield us from the pain and the shame that we are going through in our life. There is nothing more powerful than the protective love of the father that shields, protects and covers us. We must know and to understand that God's love for us is simply that we are worth fighting for. We are worth the battle. We are worth it, and he wants you to know today that you are worth it and that his love for can never be changed and that it will always remain.

When a father is fighting for his daughter or son to protect them, he will do everything within his power to ensure that they are safe and that they are loved. That is the same love that God has for us. He is will everything that he can to show us his love and to demonstrate the power and magnitude of his love for us. There are going to be attacks that we are going to be faced with, but we must keep moving and pushing towards the eternal hope and promise of God. The fight is never going to be one that is easy because God has not designed this life to be easy there are going to be challenges, trials and tests and these are to try us to help us stand strong in the faith. When it feels like the walls are caving in on you in life and that there is no room to even breathe God is waiting there to show you how much you important to him and how much he wants to see you pass your tests.

God's love for us is so gracious and he wants to demonstrate the power of his love to us in so many ways. He can't always reveal why he is doing something or why something is happening. We must trust him and acknowledge that there is something greater that is taking place and that his love for me is protecting me from the situation that I am in right now. I have had so many issues in my life in relationships and not trusting the men in my life that I was dating before I got married. I ended up getting caught up in situations that could have been handled a lot better than they were had I been obedient to God at the time.

Sometimes we are rushing to satisfy our feelings and feel like we must have something and in all actuality we don't we just think that we must have it and its not God's will for our lives. That has happened to me so much in my life that I felt the need to keep up and I ended up wrecking my life by doing things that were foolish and not seeking God about his true purpose and will for my life. When I fell prey to the things of the world and stopped being in the face of God that is where confusion stepped in and the enemy tried to deceive me into believing a lie. I had to run for my life. I prayed and asked God for a way of escape.

In the Bible it states that God will provide a way of escape for us when we are faced with temptation and God has done this for me numerous times. I don't take for granted the love that God has extended and shown to me when I have wanted to be selfish and be about myself. God waited for me with open arms because I am his chosen daughter and he has chosen to love and accept me for who I am in all my flaws and failures and mishaps. The powerful thing about God is that he already knew that these things were going to happen long before they took place and he was there to comfort me when I went through my season of darkness. A lot of people seeing me smiling and never know on the inside the pain and the turmoil that I have encountered inside.

They never know the true meaning as to why I can smile now and why I can rejoice but I have been fighting hard to let the world know of God's love for me. He rescued me from myself and that is a testimony in itself because we often feel like we have to have a certain image or be this person that people are looking for us to be and God is just waiting for us to be transparent and to open to his love and his promise for our lives. There have been many deep struggles in my life that I have battled some that I have never even talked about to family, friends or my inner circle. There have been so many secrets that I have kept to myself because I have not gotten to the place in my life that I can be fully vulnerable or to trust someone else.

When I first got married, I kept all my stuff in my car because I was so used to something bad happening from my past that I was expecting it to happen. When we wait for the bad to come it will come and it hit us hard in the face when it comes. I have always had a poor image on what love was and although I have been able to love others I have not been able to love them to the extent that I should due to past hurts that I have been holding on and not letting go of. I have been in fear of really being myself to others because of what I thought I would look like to them so I've hidden parts of my life because I never felt like I had someone that I could trust.

The whole time that I had been experiencing this God has waiting for me with open arms ready to embrace me and ready to hug the pain away that I had been going through and that I am still going through as I am writing this book. I made wrong decisions that I am well aware of and I did not seek God properly as I should and this is very dangerous because had I sought the Lord none of the things that I went through would never have taken place and God would have been there to protect my purity and my purpose. There is no greater love than the love that God has for us. His love heals the very deep parts that we are unable to get to. It reaches down to the roots and pulls out every part that we thought we had to tuck away and every part that we thought people would hate us for.

God heals and he forgives us through the power of his love. The love of Jesus is so profound in that even when we feel that what we have done in life is unforgivable that he steps in to show us that it can and it shall be forgive and that he does not even remember what we did. God is not sitting around ready to bash up upside our heads for every mistake that we make but he is there is help us and to love us through the shame and the pain that we have experienced to embrace us with his love that goes farther than we can ever imagine. Sometimes I wish I could simply go back in time in change things that I have done but I must live with it and forgive and forget.

Nothing is more powerful than knowing that God is taking care of this and it's going to be okay. It is the reassurance of knowing that he has it all under control and that he is fighting on our behalf. I am excited about God fighting on my behalf and raising me up to be a warrior woman for his Glory and not for my own. I know and understand now that there is no mistake that is too big or too small that can hinder me from God's love for my life. I have learned that in fighting for my life that the word of God has been my greatest weapon of defense and the next has been his love. Without God's love there would be no way that I could face the battle and the challenges that have been placed before me. His love has increased my awareness of how important I am to him and how far his love will go to save and to protect me from myself.

I have learned from being in the fight of my life that there is hope for my life and there is so much more to the future ahead of than I can ever imagine. I have been holding back myself from fully evolving and becoming the woman of God that he has called me to be and now I am coming of my cocoon of fear and blossoming to the butterfly that God has called. To the eagle that he has called, to the great warrior that he has called, to the Apostolic woman that he chosen me to be, I evolve into the being that he has called me to be and my fight for my life is then the fight to take all of those components and center them into one and then to soar for God. In doing so it creates my freedom and deliverance to be all that God has created me to be and more. It helps me to understand that I am never fighting this fight alone and that God is always in my corner fighting for me to help as I overcome my challenges and to receive more of his love in my life as I continue to remain steadfast and dedicated to the purpose that he has called me to and not my own. I have had surgeries in my life and have understood how easy it is to fight for your life at times and how easy it is to not fight for our lives. God is in control. He has the final say over our lives. I had to learn to let go of my control in my love life. I had to learn how to let go of the feeling that I felt that people that loved me were out to harm me in some way. This was not always the case because I had to learn how to receive and to accept love. I have never been a person that fights or purposely hurts others. I've been more of a peacemaker. My fight for my life has been in the sense that nothing was just handed to me that I had to fight for my education, I had to fight for my religion, I had to fight for what I believed in. I had to fight for my life that God has called me into and most recently I have had to fight for my name.

God has blessed me with so much in my life and at times I have taken it for granted and have not shown the appreciation that was needed at the time for the things that I had in life. At times I didn't even cherish it because I knew that I would have to someone fight to keep what it was that I was receiving in my life. The anointing of God of my life has been one that I have been fighting to endure and to protect. I know that God has hand selected me from my mother's womb to be a Prophetess to the nations and the devil hates this and he has been trying to destroy my life in the process. By trying to confuse my way of thinking towards love and trying to cause me to not to believe in love it has caused me a lot of pain in my life.

In my life walk with God I have to remember that I have to keep fighting in the process but at the same time remember that the battle is solely the Lords and that he has the final say over what is happening and not me. Yes, it's imperative to fight for what and who we love and its imperative to stand strong in our faith in God's love for us and know that his love is forever fighting for us and that he truly has our backs when it comes to love.

I could not fully embrace God's love and accept his fighting on my behalf without first recognizing that I was worth fighting for. It has taken me some months now to recover from shame and from the hurt that I have experienced in my life. I didn't want to start writing again until I felt like and really knew that healing had taken place in my life. Sometimes it's easy to picture being completely healed of something and then when it happens it is so rewarding. God has helped me to learn how to unmask the camouflaging in my life that I thought I had to do. He has helped to expose the places in my life that needed the most healing. I didn't realize the suppressed anger and unforgiveness that I had held in my heart for my father being absent in my life. I have since then began to build a relationship and talk to my father, but it took me years to get to that place. I had to learn to stop blaming him for what I had been through in my life and to learn to love and forgive him. My perception of my father was causing my love for my father God to be hard because I had to learn what a loving father was like.

I am learning now that I cannot be angry forever at things that I had no control over. God's love for my life has helped me to heal and it has helped me to understand so much more about myself and my identity in Christ. When I came to know who I truly was in Christ I then knew how important it was for God to fight for me. I knew that there was no way possible for me to continue to push away or to refuse the love of Jesus fighting for me in my life. For so long I put up a I am showing that I was okay but deep down inside I was not okay, and I had to learn how to express this. When I was not okay, I had to learn how to vocalize this and communicate this in a manner that did not hurt or affect others but at the same time I needed to release it from ever happening again

in my life.

Chapter Four

Real Love

There is nothing more beautiful than real love. We often see couples and we see the sparkle in their eyes for the one that they love, and we see the true love has found them and that they are happy. That is real love. Real love shows and everyone knows that you love the person because it's just that real to you that you want everyone to know about it. Real love is like that in our relationship with Jesus. His love for us pours out daily on our lives. We experience a love like that of married couple. God loves for us is for forever and we have all the benefits included in love in that relationship. Love has found me in my most broken places in my life and it has propelled me to want more of God's love.

Each day I am expectant of God's love and I want to experience more of his love because it's just that genuine. I have had fears of love and fear of failure in love, but I am learning now how to receive the love that God has intended for my life for so long. I am in great anticipation of more of God's love because it continues to overshadow me, and it helps me to be the woman that

I am now and the woman that I am becoming. God's love for us is different in that it is not earned he just gives it to us.

We don't have to convince him to love us he just loves us because we are just that special to him and wants to show us how valuable we are to him. I have had my share of counterfeits with love in the past with men that I have dated, and it always took me longer to look beyond the butterflies in my stomach and to acknowledge real and true love. True love is not intended to hurt or harm you on purpose but to push you into your destiny. Sometimes the real can be staring right at us and we are too blind to see it. That is how God's love is for us.

Real love is not disguised it is open and it available and it is so real that it is shown in the way that we speak, and the way that we treat others. When we take on the image of Christ as a new believer, we embrace that new love in our lives.

Real love which comes from God can't fail and God's love never lies to us. He wants the best for our loves and his job is to cover us with his love. Real love extends beyond the pain that we have in our hearts and it begins to mend the broken areas. Real love uncovers that pain that is deep in the bottom of our hearts not to destroy us but to bring us to a place of peace in knowing that survival is attainable and that nothing can ever replace the love of God. The day that I experienced the true love of Jesus and there was several times before this but the day that I had an eye opening experience was when I was in church and there was this beautiful worship song being sung by Hillsong called you loved me as you found me.

It just gripped my heart and bought me to tears because God saw my mess, he saw my pain he saw my shame and despite it all he loved me where he found me. I had been in some low places in my life and God has always been waiting for me with open arms to ensure me that it's going to be alright and he is my healer. God's love is so real that it erases the painful memories that we once had, and God puts it all in the sea of forgetfulness. The power of real love is like a rare gem its valuable and there is a distinction in that shows its genuineness. Real love also produces action. Real love has real results that are fruitful. The real love that God has for us is one that we can boast and share to others about. In Romans 12:9 it states that, "Love must be sincere. Hate what is evil; cling to what is good. [10] Be devoted to one another in love. Honor one another above yourselves.[11] Never be lacking in zeal, but keep your spiritual fervor, serving the Lord. [12] Be joyful in hope, patient in affliction, faithful in prayer. [13] Share with the Lord's people who are in need. Practice hospitality.[14] Bless those who persecute you; bless and do not curse. [15] Rejoice with those who rejoice; mourn with those who mourn. [16] Live in harmony with one another. Do not be proud but be willing to associate with people of low position. Do not be conceited. [17] Do not repay anyone evil for evil. Be careful to do what is right in the eyes of everyone. [18] If it is possible, as far as it depends on you, live at peace with everyone. [19] Do not take revenge, my dear friends, but leave room for God's wrath, for it is written: "It is mine to avenge; I will repay," says the Lord. [20] On the contrary: "If your enemy is hungry, feed him;

if he is thirsty, give him something to drink. In doing this, you will hear burning coals on his head." [21] Do not be overcome by evil but overcome evil with good."

The important thing to remember always real love is that it speaks for itself. When love is real it causes you to draw more deeply and closer to the one that you love and that is how a relationship with God is. It helps you to move closer to Jesus and to want to experience his love for us because in finding his love for us we also find hope. I don't know how many of you are reading this today and you are experiencing hopelessness in your life and you are going through depression. God wants to pour his love on you and show you his real love. His love can't be copied because his love is the real thing and it does not get better than that.

Real love is just that its real and when its real it can affect the hearts of those around us as well. When Jesus asked his disciples, who touched me he felt the virtue go out of him. The woman's faith had reached him, and her faith gave her healing. Some of us God does not have to touch because our faith has already touched him. So is the great love of God for us. His real love for us extends to us in such a way that are assured of his love because he has never shown us anything different. Real love is not conniving or sneaky its love that is pure and has not hidden agendas in mind.

In Romans 13:8 it states that, "[8] Owe no man anything, but to love one another: for he that loveth another hath fulfilled the law." Real love covers the debts and penalties that happened before hand. Real love moves the mountains of our doubts and replaces it with faith. Real love takes the fear inside of us that has been holding us back and replaces it with love. When God removes something in our lives it is not to harm or hurt us because it to give us what he knows is best for us at the time. Real love chastens us in such a way the edifies us and then at the same time aligns us to stay on the right path with God.

Real love also empowers us to become better in lives. Real love is not looking for a stage or a platform to show off but its waiting for us always. God wants to reveal more of his love for us and he is waiting for us to accept his love and to embrace the real outpouring of his love for us. When we truly open our hearts to God and not just on Easter Sunday when everyone is speaking about love or on Valentine's day when everyone is getting an I love you balloon and flowers. Real love is so much greater than one day. God wants to show us that in his real love its being poured in such a way that we can affect change in the lives of others because of the power of the love of our father Jesus inside of us.

Real love goes deeper than any love that we can ever imagine. Experiencing the true love of Jesus is just like that we must go deeper in our relationship with God to experience the deep love that he has for our lives. Going deeper in God means pulling away, fasting, spending time with God and communicating with God more in prayer. Real love is not just what we can get or what gift that God can give. He is going to bless us and shower us with gifts because he is that great of a God, he will do that, but he wants to show us that love is so much more than material things.

What I have discovered in the love of God is that its complete and it's not looking for avenues to find completion it is simply complete. One of the things that I have been looking for is validation from others. I thought that the only way to rise was to constantly be doing something and being a part of something to feel loved. I had developed an addiction to being approved and validated by others and it became so toxic that I felt at times numb until someone say it was good what I had done or what I had accomplished. I had built my whole life on accomplishing goals to seek and receive love from others. I had no recollection at the time that this was not a way to real love, but it was a way to continue in a rollercoaster cycle like a rat spinning on wheel going no fast. If my next high was found in someone saying that something that I did helped them then that meant more to me that anything. God showed me that my validation and worth was not found in others, but my validation was found in him.

I didn't have to put on shows or act anymore that I can simply be myself and that he loved me just as I was. In Ephesians 2:10 it says that, "For we are God's masterpiece. He has created us anew in Christ Jesus so we can do the good things that he planned for us long ago." When God looks at us, he does not just look at us see, Monique, or Billy, or Sue but he sees his masterpiece. His beautiful masterpiece that he has created and predestined for such a time as time that is shining for his glory. He sees his marvelous creation that he has made that is now an image for his kingdom.

The thing that we must always understand about the real love of Jesus is that it's just that real. Nothing can imitate it or manipulate it because the real love of God is pure and from it is all the validation that you will ever need in life. In the Father's love is grace, peace, joy, understanding and fulfillment. Real love captures the very epilogue that you have been awaiting!

Chapter Five

Love never fails

According to Merriam Webster Dictionary, the word failure is defined as, "**omission** of occurrence or performance. A state of inability to perform a normal function. Lack of success. An abrupt cessation of normal functioning, deterioration or decay." When I look at this definition it shows negative words that are never carried through. I don't see any of the attributes of Jesus in this definition. The love of Jesus is none of the words that depict failure, but the love of Jesus is infinitely more than our failures. In fact, his love *NEVER* fails! Yes, that is correct *NEVER*. We may be waiting for a failure to happen in Christ but it's not going to happen because God love is true in that it does not fail. In Psalm 73:26 it says, "My health may fail, and my spirit may grow weak, but God remains the strength of my heart; he is mine forever."

I want you take a piece of paper out and write the words things that I have failed on one side and then on the other side write things that God has done for me. From this exercise you will see that God's love for you outweighs all your failures. You can write all day about what you did not accomplish or complete but God's love reigns supreme. Sometimes we overcomplicate God's love for us but it his love is simple and extravagant at the same time. Coming from a background of abuse and suffering I had to learn how to channel my hurt and my feelings and a lot of times this caused me to hold a lot of things in and to never talk about them. I never knew how much harm that I was doing to myself mentally, physically and spiritually by doing this. I was causing pain and affliction on myself and was not even aware of the danger it was causing to my life. We are oftentimes our worst critics, and this is so true and real. I had a hard time embracing love because of the distorted image that I had given to myself that love was equivalent to pain and that I did not deserve to be loved or to be cared for because it would only bring harm to my life.

The more that I started studying the scriptures and listening to sound wisdom and hearing from God it then helped to capture what was causing blockage in my life and how to open the pain and let it all out to fully recover. The only way to reach deeply inside of what has been affecting us is to get to the root or the core and then correct it. For some people it takes years to this because of how deeply the pain has been rooted into our lives. That was what I had been experiencing for so long the suppressed pain was causing me to believe that love was going to fail me too and that I had nothing to look forward to. In my family line there was so much divorce and I had a fear of love. A part of me wanted to have security and control. I didn't know how to let go of my fears and give to give it all to God. Although I was speaking it from my mouth the action was being delayed. I realized that I had to fall in love with God for myself not for my family, friends, or pastor but for myself. I realized that the only way to do this was to get real with God and to get real with myself.

I could no longer hide behind the shadows of my fears, but it was now time to embrace the unfailing love of Jesus. He is my protector and my everything. In Psalm 143:8 it says that, "Let me hear of your unfailing love each morning, for I am trusting you. Show me where to walk, for I give myself to you." This scripture helped to capture me in a place of surrender and to say to God each morning that I give myself to you. I am not looking for love because the Lord that you have given has already found me. We can sometimes waste time on trying to replace and find love in our lives when God is standing there waiting for us and showing us his love the whole time. Why are we blocking love when love has come to heal us? Why are we blocking love when love has come to transform us? Why do we push God away when he is so near and dear to our lives?

We need the love that God has for us. We need the love that he is giving to us daily because it refreshes us, it cleanses us, it restores us, and it replenishes us. We may have had fathers or father figures in our lives that have failed us or that have not been there for us as we have intended and maybe this has blocked you from believing in love again or maybe it has caused you to have a wall in your life like I have that I did not know until my 30's that I was holding on to and that I am just now coming to release.

Falling in Love with Jesus

When I ponder on a love that is unfailing, I imagine comfort and peace but at the same time I also imagine so much grace and gratitude from the love that it brings. There is so much assurance from the love that God shows and demonstrates to us in that is has a trademark of acceptance. God wants to extend that trademark to us and place the brand of his approval over us that we are loved and that he is never going to fail us. God has been that ultimate love to me that I have longed to have. I longed for so very long ago to not look or to expect my love from people but to hold true to what was real in my life and the only real love that I have known has been God's love. It has been most monumental in implementing the meaning of compassion and forgiveness.

In his compassion that he delivers to me it is one that speaks volumes to my life. It is one that I one to hold over me forever and to embrace. I have heard of many other religions but the one that stands true is Christianity and the love that God has for his children. There are many people that blame God and that hate God because things are not going their way and they have not come to build a real relationship with God. We must know that our relationship with God may not always be popular for others, but we must know and realize the power of God in our lives and his love overshadowing the doubts of others that fail to believe. I try not force my beliefs on others but what I will do is share the love relationship that I have with others and allow them the choice of experiencing it for themselves and discovering the truth of God's love for their lives.

For so long I have met many people that have turned a cold shoulder to me because of my relationship with God. That shows me that I am in a place with God that has me shielded and protected. Many may not understand why I love God the way that I do and why I can remain confident in the love that he has for my life that never fails. But it is evident to me that what I am experiencing through God's love is real and that the purity in it will breathe wholeness to others that I encountered.

I remember when I first got saved all that I could talk about was Jesus. It was the most beautiful experience of my life. I got saved at a shut in and there a room full of church mothers that were seeking the lord and praying all night. I never know that was what

God wanted to show me early on that I too was chosen and that I was a prayer warrior. He wanted to show me that his love for me would never fail. He began to reveal that to me years later but as a child I remember having dreams about the beauty of God and now seeing the fulfillment of the promises that he had given to me so many years ago.

Vulnerability and transparency are something that I have now grown to appreciate and to value. It was not something that I utilized in my life because I had built a wall that no one was ever to unlock. I had purposely built the wall because I was afraid of being vulnerable and I was afraid of making a mistake and messing up. I was afraid of who I was becoming, and I felt like I had a sense of control when I was dictating this wall in my life. I would only allow people to get a limited closeness to my life. There was so many people that I loved but pushed away on purpose and I often regret this because their intentions were well but because of my feelings on how I thought love should be I pushed them away and closed the door. I felt like in doing that it would give me the upper hand, but it really didn't it just gave me more pain and grief from not allowing myself to be transparent and to be vulnerable to those who were close to me at the time.

Sometimes it takes being vulnerable to really understand the heart of someone or an issue that has be placed before us. When we become vulnerable, we then expose the power of real love and embrace it. It takes trust and trust can only be established when we are vulnerable enough to give the trust to another person. If we don't know how to trust someone then it becomes hard to develop that level of love and companionship with them or intimacy. Not intimacy in a sexual manner but intimacy in closeness.

Vulnerability brings that closeness to our lives that we need. I have been one that has told myself numerous times that I did not need someone or something but what does is produce pride and not love. When we will feel like we don't need people because we have been hurt that is a dangerous place to be in because it causes us to become secluded and place trust only in ourselves and not in others.

We need to understand that when God says that his love never fails that it is his love that never fails and not our love. We as human beings fail one another, and we often hurt each other. It is a part of life it is a part of us getting to know one another and building and establishing that trust in the other person. We are bound to make mistakes and to mess up, but it should not be habitual patterns. The love of God dwells inside of us and exhibits his attributes. As Christians we are given the love of God and his love is not just for us but for all of humanity. He hates the sin, but he loves the person. He does not hate us. God loves us and wants to see become all that he has designed and created us to be in this hour. I want to make a difference in this world and God's love is helping me to do that and I am going after God more than I ever have before because he is my first love and his has shown me that his love for me is real and that its unfailing and that I have to want more of his love for my life daily. The way that I have learned to do so if spending more time with God and now even writing to God has be phenomenal, he has endless love for me.

Chapter Six

Dr. Monique Vann

Embracing the beauty of God's love

For so long my equation of beauty and love was limited to that of surface belief. I had been in modeling school before at John Casablanca's and I modeled for stores and took pictures. Beauty was in no comparison to the beauty and love that God had for my life. His love goes beyond surface and vanity and empties me out of my love for self and puts a new level on love on my life called sacrifice one that as a single I had to learn how to activate and as a married one I had to learn how to give back in but did exercise or utilize any of it well. My struggle started years ago in my teens when I was thirteen years old until I was in my mid-twenties, I suffered with eating disorders because I had a distorted view of how my self-image should resemble and how beauty is to be displayed to others. I thought that if I could lose weight that everything would change for my life and that everything would be better.

I was under the impression that my acceptance had to come from my physical appearance and that if I was beautiful and looked good that everything would be okay. But this was truly a lie from the enemy. My beauty in Christ is not about the outer in anyway but the inward in my life needed to show the true of God's heart and his love for me. When I allowed the beauty that world system said that I have to have to invade my life I then set myself up to believe that beauty then was only surfaced and that there was no beauty beyond that which is not true at all. I love a song by Mandisa called True Beauty. When we have true beauty in our lives it exemplifies the beauty of Jesus.

Embracing the beauty of God's love is the same in that in his love for us it catapults us to extraordinary love. The extent that God went to help me to realize that surfaced love was never enough was truly an eye opener for me. I am thankful to God for blessing me with beauty but at the same time I also wanted to have the humility that comes with that and the only way to find that is through letting go of the surfaced love and moving in God's love for my life. I had this preconceived notion of what love should look like to me and how I should look when it came to love someone else. I had the beauty needed to catch a man but what I needed most was the heart to really keep him. That was something that I lacked because I thought at times that I was entitled to certain things and that I should have them. I was the baby girl in my family, so it then caused me to be spoiled.

The Bible speaks about sparing the rod spoiling the child. I have had my share of spankings and I was physically abused by my stepfather who is now deceased. It was very painful. It was so hard to go to church on Sundays because he was a minister in the church at the time and see him love and embrace people and then go home to be tortured and abused was beyond what I could possibly imagine. I thought to myself this cannot be love this is not what the father's love looks or feels like. It should not always be pain. I had to learn how to embrace the beauty of God's love. Being seven years old I had not yet mastered that yet. I was still learning about salvation and how deeply important I want to be saved, baptized and filled with the Holy Ghost.

I wanted something deeper in my life and at the time I had no idea that I was preparing myself for the future as a minister of the Gospel. I had no idea at the time what I was setting myself up to become. I just knew I did not want the pain in my life that myself, my sister, and my mom were enduring. It became in that

cycle that abuse would then move throughout my family. My mom

was physically abused, my sister was physically abused and then I

was physically abused. We all ended up getting involved with me

that harmed us and hurt us. When I became older, I had become

involved with men and women that hurt me and abused me. I

didn't understand early on in my life that suppressed hurt and pain

would lead me to do things that were ungodly. I had not come to

the true knowledge of God's love for me yet and I was desperate to

find his love for my life. I have so many regrets in my life for my

past, but I am thankful for the freedom and deliverance that God

had brought to my life. I want to keep that freedom and walk in its

daily to help others to know that there is so much to life than

abuse, pain and torture. I also want them to know that they do not

have stay where they have begun but there is a greater promise of

love for their lives. There is a greater promise of God's love that

they can now experience. Romans 8:35 says, "For I am persuaded

that neither death nor life, nor angels nor principalities nor powers,

nor things present nor things to come, nor height nor depth, nor any other created thing, shall be able to separate us from

the love of God which is in Christ Jesus our Lord."

In Psalm 33:18 it says, "I have loved you, my people, with

an everlasting love. With unfailing love, I have drawn you to

myself." Psalm 32:10 goes on to say that, "The Word became

human and lived here on earth among us. He was full of unfailing

love and faithfulness. And we have seen his glory, the glory of the

only Son of the Father." In John 3:16 it says, "God so loved the

world that he gave his only Son, so that everyone who believes in

him will not perish but have eternal life. God did not send his Son

into the world to condemn it, but to save it." I could go on and on

about the scriptures about God's word for our lives. To understand

and to appreciate the way that God loves we must picture and

imagine what beauty looks like beyond a royal crown, makeup,

and shiny shoes and makeup. What does beauty that is real look

like? It is flawed or is it bruised? Real beauty constitutes just that it

is in the beauty of God that we are loved forever more and

treasured.

One of my favorite scriptures in Corinthians about love says that, "1 Corinthians 13:4-8:

- Love is Patient, Love is Kind; Love does envy, Love does not boast; Love is not arrogant

- Love is not rude. Love does not insist on its own way; Love is not irritable or resentful

- Love does not rejoice at wrongdoing but rejoices with the truth

- Love bears all things, Love believes all things, Love hopes all things, Love endures all things

- Love NEVER ends or fails."

How beautiful is that! That God's love for us not only contains beauty that is defined in him and that covers us, but it also has beauty that pours out continuously. In Ephesians 2:4-7 it says that, "May you experience the love of Christ, though it is so great you will never fully understand it. Then you will be filled with the fullness of life and power that comes from God." Ephesians 3:19 goes on to tell us that, "Anyone who does not love does not know God – for God is love. God showed how much he loved us by sending his only Son into the world so that we might have eternal life through him.

This is real love. It is not that we loved God, but that he loved us and sent his Son as a sacrifice to take away our sins. Dear friends, since God loved us that much, we surely ought to love each other. No one has ever seen God. But if we love each other, God lives in us, and his love has been brought to full expression through us. And God has given us his Spirit as proof that we live in him and he in us. There is nothing that we can do that can change the beauty of God's love for us. This has given me tremendous peace and assurance because it depicts a more gratifying and accepted love that I never knew would exist in my life. One that was not controlled or forced but instead welcomed. God will never force himself on us or do something to harm us intentionally. He loves his children and he wants to see us rising into our purpose and he wants us to know the beauty that he has for us and liberate us to the beauty by opening our hearts, minds, ears, eyes to see all the love of God that is around us through others and through his great love for us. God's love is always going to win in our lives because he has the final say over our lives. God's love for us is so instrumental in that creates a deeper longing for more of his love.

My friends and I would joke sometimes when we messed up and say that we need to have a coming to Jesus moment. Now, those words remain supreme in my life because it's no longer a joke love with Jesus is real and my love for him is real and his love for me is real. I now know that I cannot play around when it comes to love and that I must either be in or out. In Revelation 3:16 it says in the New Living Translation, "But since you are like lukewarm water, neither hot nor cold, I will spit you out of my mouth!" We may think what beauty is that when someone is willing to spit us out of their mouths. But that is how serious God wants us to be with our relationship with him because he does not want us to be lukewarm in our love or in our relationship with him.

I had to find the beauty in Christ in my relationship with him. God's love for my life has helped me to see the power that love has in all aspects of my life. It may take people years to see love for real and for some its instant. We never have to worry about being blinded in God's love because its real and there is so much authenticity in it that it captures the memories that we never even knew existed.

Chapter Seven

Love Chisels

I can't write a book about love without creating awareness that love chastens. When I think of chastening, I think of a chisel that is shaping the sides to ensure that it is shaped accordingly and that the all the edges are smooth. That is how the love of Jesus must chisel us. At times we may have things that are out of order in our lives that need realignment and chiseling. What the love of father does then is it chisels us so much to the extent that its painful but only for a short while. I have had many points in my life that feel like a small chisel is shaping me and molding me and shaping me to the place that I need to be in God. Chisel according to Merriam Webster is defined as, "a metal tool with a sharpened edge at one end used to chip, carve, or cut into a solid material (such as wood, stone, or metal)"

Chiseling that does not have to always have a negative connotation. It can represent what has not been cored or tamed in our lives. The things that stick out and hinder us from our destiny of being the men and women of God that we should be. It hurts while it is being done and that is what Jesus does to us at times in the spirit, he prepares us for the chisel and helps us to know that he is cutting off the things in our lives that have smothered our purpose. He is cutting off the cords that have kept us tangled in bondage to ourselves and to others. He is shaping off the things that have blocked us from maintaining our relationship with God. The chisel represents the sign of chastening that comes with love. When God corrects us, it is not to harm us or to punish us in such a way that he gets rid of us and no longer has use of us. His love instead protects us and covers us to show us that we think that we need at the time is harmful and he will remove it in order to protect us and to cover us.

In the word of God, it says that whom the Lord loves that he chastens. His love is not like someone enduring a beating.

For whom the LORD loves He chastens,

And scourges every son whom He receives."

[7] If you endure chastening, God deals with you as with sons; for what son is there whom a father does not chasten? [8] But if you are without chastening, of which all have become partakers, then you

are illegitimate and not sons. [9] Furthermore, we have had human

fathers who corrected *us,* and we paid *them* respect. Shall we not

much more readily be in subjection to the Father of spirits and

live? [10] For they indeed for a few days chastened *us* as

seemed *best* to them, but He for *our* profit, that *we* may be

partakers of His holiness. [11] Now no chastening seems to be joyful

for the present, but painful; nevertheless, afterward it yields the

peaceable fruit of righteousness to those who have been trained by

it. Chastening is set in place as a sign of love and care for the

other.

As a school teacher I have had to maintain firmness and

directness in the classroom to maintain order and discipline and

God's love is the same way in that his love directs us and guides us

but at the same time it also disciplines us to show us that he cares

about us. When someone truly loves that other person, they will do

all that they can to tell them when they are doing right and when

they are doing wrong. Love celebrates the good and corrects the

bad in order to prevent harm from occurring.

When the things that have been done wrong have been exposed and are rectified it can create healing and deliverance in our lives. There have been times in my life that I know that I should have not had grace in a situation but God's love shielded and protected me and helped me to see and to recognize that if it was not for his love where would I be and if was not for his love how then would I make it. His love was a sign to me that I am here, and I have the best for you, but I had to want the best for my life. I had to love myself enough to want to be loved and I had to love myself enough to corrected and to be chiseled so that I could walk in the path that God was leading me in. In some instances, God has had to chisel even the path that I was walking on so that I would be protected and safe from the path that I was going down. I remember so many times in my life where fitting in was so hard because of the call of God on my life but I had to know that I was chosen and that I could not do the things that others people were doing and get away with them.

Even when I tried to hide I couldn't because God would send someone to correct me or to tell me where I was wrong and how to fix it. I grew up in a church that everyone knew your name and your family. I had always had a conscience about protecting my family name and it was instilled in me at a young age to this but as I got older because I was sheltered so much I began to rebel in my teens and run away from home and not come back. I realized now that I was running away from myself because I was afraid of the purpose that God had for my life and I was afraid of doing what I was supposed to because I wanted to fit in with the crowd.

As I got older in my twenties, I found myself drinking and hanging out in places that I would never imagine myself going into. I had transitioned to a life that I had never imagined that I would enter. I connected with men that I should not have been involved with and I even had a sugar daddy to ensure that my money never ran out. This was not the life that God wanted for me. I was in a stage of rebellion in my life because I thought I would fit in and be accepted if I did these things. I felt so ashamed and remorseful after these things happened in myself. I felt myself going around in circles in my life it seemed I was not really living the life that God intended for my life because I was so busy trying to please and appease others and I was afraid of the word no. I didn't realize then that God's was chiseling me to say the word no that I had no strength to even speak at the time. He loved me so much that he saw my shame and ugliness and the sin that I was in. He saw my backslidden condition and he saw where I was going and not where I was at. I could only see the pain and the shame now, but God loved me beyond where I was because I was just that important to him and the call on my life was so much greater than what I could possibly imagine. It took a lot of long hard nights of struggle, homelessness, abuse and shame to wake me up to see the love that God had for my life and to open my eyes and my heart and receive it.

I had been so accustomed to pushing love away that I knew how to love emptied. I don't even know how that is possible, but it was very painful for me. I have learned how to reconstruct my life now in such a way that it has become pleasing to God. I realized that my life was not one of perfection that I wanted it to be and that was okay. For so long I had dreamed of being married and having lots of children that I had never once stopped to really ask

God was this what he wanted for my life or was I trying to fit in to be accepted. God loved me when I was single, and he also loved me when I was married.

He loved me in all my mistakes. The chisel for me that God brought to my life helped to save me from myself and to keep stretching to keep pushing for his love in my life and to get rid of every desire of the world that I thought I had to have. I was deceived thinking that I had to live a certain way and I didn't. I had to follow the way that was right and that was the way of God and holiness and purity. My life took a complete change between 2017 and 2018. So much had shifted and taken place. Now in 2019, I see God arising in my life in such a way to show me that he has the ultimate chisel for my life, and he wants to shake me and break me from the things that have caused me to be stagnant. He wants to shape me and mold me into the woman of God that he has created. God must scrape off and remove the things that are side tracking us from our purpose to reveal to us his love for us. When he chisels us it may not happen every day but when it happens there is something great that God wants to reveal to us in our lives and he has to go deep inside and chisel it out in order to get rid of it from destroying our lives. He must chisel away things that have started to create decay in our lives and remove it so that it does not bring any more harm to our lives.

The chisel is sharp, and it hurts when God speaks his word and his truth to us its real and it sometimes will cause of to cry because of the realness that is attached to what he is trying to do in our lives. There is such a great work that he wants us to do and we must complete it. The chiseling helps us to stay sharp in God and to truly hear his voice and to hear what he is saying to us. The chisel also prepares us to experience the pain of going deeper and how the sharpness is eluded to the deeper things in God. I know that I cannot look to be like others or my friends or family, but I must look to be whom God has created me to be. If he must chisel me every day, I want God to help me to break away from myself and from my needs to fulfill his purpose in this life. The deeper that I allow God to cut to the core and chasten me to grow its going to help me to mature into the things of him.

I can't grow in God by staying in the same place that I was in years ago but I have to know within my spirit that there is so much more that God wants to bring to my life and there is so much that he wants to empty out of me that that I can be completely free. That is true and ultimate love a love that sees us when we are in wrong and does something about to shape in a way that does not harm ourselves or harm others. Will you allow God to chisel you today? Will you allow him to get to the core of your hurt and pain in your hearts and begin to pull it out? Will you allow God to begin to cut away what is not needed in your life and what is not producing the God kind of fruit that you need in your life. Allow God to chisel you today because it is in the chiseling that his love is shown. Each day is not always roses and sunshine that we live in because God has to get the ugly things out of our lives to make us better and taking us through a pruning and healing process that is going to allow us to get rid of the pain in our lives. When we have been chiseled by the master it is a sign that love stands corrected and that he wants to correct and change some things inside of us.

We have to know that it is not always an easy process when we decide to get back on the right path with God but we have to continue growing and allowing him to chisel out the things in our lives that are there so that it can make us better. We are made better when we can accept correction from God. Not in a way that comes to destroy us but in a way that comes to renew us and bring true deliverance to our lives. We must keep going and expect the chastening to come in the form of a chisel from God and accept it. The chiseling has not been designed to destroy us but to make us better in God in all areas of our lives.

In this season I have experienced the power of God in my life and I have experienced God healing me. I have also experienced God delivering me. But one of the greatest things that I have now learned to appreciate is God chiseling me to help me to become free of myself. Sometimes we become so far into what we are doing that God has to come in and help us to strip away the things that are hurting us to help us to no longer be entangled with them. We must become stretched in such a way that we know that we cannot live comfortably in sin, shame or disobedience. Sin becomes a simple gratification that we feel and experience and then we end up going after the gratification again to help us to ease the pain in our lives. I was guilty of this. I kept gravitating to what was harmful for my life because I felt like there was some sort of security in it but there wasn't. The chiseling from God helped me to become aware of and to recognize that there was so much power within my life that I had given to others and to the enemy that needed to be relinquished because it was causing my life to become stagnated. I thank God for stripping me away of things that were most harmful to my life and replacing it with things that were most beneficial to my life. I have always known and recognized that I wanted more in life and that I could never be a person that just settled and accepted mediocrity in my life.

God is speaking this to you in this season that you must stop allowing the mediocrity to take control of your life and tap into the excellence that he wants to bring in your life. He wants to bring you to freedom and joy and into a place of complete surrender and peace in doing the will of God for your life. Allow the chiseling to begin in order that your life will be made better through the power of change and transformation in your life. A transformation must take place in order that God can really heal and deliver us from what is happening in our lives. I had to learn to accept the transformation that was taking place in my life. I had to recently go to Pensacola Florida to receive the impartation that I was supposed to have received 10 years ago. Can you imagine waiting ten years for something that God had promised to you. The process took longer because I had allowed myself to get wrapped up in things and with people that I should not have been involved with and it hindered me from my promise. What should have taken me 22 years to receive it took me longer because I was not able to hear God properly and I allowed myself to become distracted.

The enemy tries to catch us off guard to steal the promises that God has ordained for our lives and to try to bring shame and harm to us. God restores and one of the things that God spoke to me was that he was going to accelerate everything that I lost and give it to me in a swift moving escalator. We will never miss what God has for us because he is waiting patiently for us to receive what he has for our lives. We never have to feel like we are missing out in life or that we did not obtain all that we were supposed to. God does not want us to live our lives like we are on a roller coaster ride going as fast as possible neither does he want us to feel like everything is going to be microwaved and handed to us right away. There are times that things will be accelerated and then there are times to which God purposely does things slowly for us in order to protect us and to prepare us for what is coming.

The only way to be prepared for what is coming is to fully understand the power behind why it is coming and how important it is to our lives at the time. At this point in my life I would never have imagined myself to be where I am today and it's all because of God's love that I am where I am and I standing where I am standing. God took a girl like myself from the hood in New Jersey to living in the projects on welfare at the time and food stamps to be the first in my family to graduate with a doctorate degree. He has even blessed me now to be a math teacher at middle school. I didn't get there overnight I had to put the time in. I had to work for 9 months as a substitute teacher and wait patiently on an interview to get to the promise that God had for my life for so long. It was not a fast process although nine months to me represented the time of God birthing me fully into the full promises that he had on my life. That's the power of God's love for us he wanted to take us deeper in our finite minds than we could ever have imagined.

He wants us to know and to understand the true power of his love for our lives. He doesn't want to keep the love that he has for us boxed up but poured out on us. He wants to pour out his love and grace over our lives daily. God wants us to empty out ourselves that we may be filled with more of his love in our lives. He wants to restore the lost places in our lives and to fill each voided place with more of his love in our lives.

Chapter Eight

Daily Love Notes to God

When I first became saved, I remember writing notes to God in a small journal and placing it under my pillow. I would wait to hear answers back from God from the notes that I had written to him. Although the response was not on a written piece of paper as I expected to be as little girl I saw a response in other ways through the Bible in scriptures, through angelic messengers, through prophets, through songs, through bill boards outside and even sometimes through a license plate on a car.

God has a way of delivering messages to us in rare forms and it does it as a sign of love to us. His love notes to us are very special because he wants us to know that he truly does hear us. I have loved writing so much as a young girl I would write little comic books and sell them to friends and I would ask them to leave a small note to me afterwards and I would even include a small note of thanks to them for purchasing the book even though it was 25 cents at the time to me it seemed like 25 thousand because it was so special to me. That is how God sees our love notes to him.

He views it as being one of the most beautiful things that we can ever write.

Writing to God is so beautiful you don't have to be an author to write a love note to God it is simply an act of love that you are extending to God to show your appreciation to him and how much he means to you. It does not have to be written on fancy paper although it would be nice to present it God in excellence. It does not have to be some long drawn out letter it is simply your heartfelt thoughts to God on paper. Now with the use of technology you can take your love notes further and extend it as a voice note to God on your phone or download an app that has a notetaker on it and write daily love notes to God. You can create a small love notes diary or journal. You can go to the dollar store and get note paper or be as creative with it as you want it is your love note to God. All he wants is our whole hearts. When we give him our whole hearts, we look forward to writing love notes to God and expressing our heartfelt thoughts to him. It is something so special about pursuing God and reaching out to him and writing a love note to God is a simple form of showing love and appreciation to God for all that he has done in our lives. I write notes of gratitude and thanks and I also write notes to just say to God that I love him, and I desire more of him that an anything in this world. His love is so wonderful to me.

I know that in receiving love from God that I show my love to him by writing to him and telling him how I feel. I express to God how deeply my love has grown for him. It can never reach the magnitude of his love, but it can capture the love that I choose to share with God that is sacred and for him. I look forward to waiting up and seeking God in intercession and prayer now because there was a time that I did not do these things and it took away from my relationship with God.

I never want to be pulled away from God, but I want to grow closer to him and reach for more of him in my life and the love notes that I give to him help me to do that. It helps me to write and appreciate his love in a way that is most creative to him because I can never pay God for all that he has given to me but was a sign of gratitude and appreciation to God I can extend my thanks and gratitude in the form of a love note or letter. Like the aspect of being in love and dating. That how are our love notes are to God that are a sign to him of his great love for us. The way to build a strong relationship is to date and share thoughts and feelings towards one another. God had touched my life in such a way that I look forward to writing and sharing my thoughts with him. Like with any relationship he reigns supreme in that I treasure every moment that I get to spend with him and I look forward to every chance that I get to acknowledge how much his love means to me and how much I want others to know of his great love. My notes to God can also come in the form of a love song that I may write to him or my note may be a song that I play on my guitar that is only for me and God at the time. I often find myself writing in my car when I am at a long light to tell God how much I love him and thank God for him. That is how God is towards us he is waiting for every chance that he can to tell us how much he loves and appreciates us. He may send notes in creative ways to us to reveal how much he loves us.

One of the things that I find myself looking forward to is God's love. It is in the love notes from God that I can keep standing and breathing with assurance that his love truly prevails. God wants to see us through everything in our lives and he sees us through it when we least expect it. We must keep going realize how valuable we are to God and that his notes are simply a sign to us that love is real and that his love for us is truly real. I find myself writing notes to God in various ways and I enjoy it so much so that I end up writing love notes daily.

I am going to take the time out more often to write love notes to God because it is truly symbolic to how much I love him and thank him for being the creator of my life. I don't know where my life would have ended up without God. He waits for us so patiently and it is one of the things that I must really ponder on at times because he is so great. First Corinthians 13:1 says. "Though I speak with the tongues of men and of angels, but have not love, I have become sounding brass or a clanging cymbal. And though I have *the gift of* prophecy, and understand all mysteries and all knowledge, and though I have all faith, so that I could remove mountains, but have not love, I am nothing. And though I bestow all my goods to feed *the poor,* and though I give my body to be burned, but have not love, it profits me nothing. Having love in our loves that is true for God produces the love that we need in our lives to keep moving forward. God is not sitting around and thinking about how he can love us he has created us to love us and for us to love him. When we come to truly love to accept and embrace the love of God it causes us to gravitate to him and to pursue him. We don't want our love for him to clank and not be heard but we want our love to be heard and that God will listen to what we are asking or saying at the time. One of things that I enjoy about writing love notes to God is that he hears us, and he listens to us when we are not even listening. He doesn't want anything to come in between the love that he has for us. God is a jealous God and he will not have any idols before him. If there are things in your life that have replaced God's love that you once had for him or has come in the way of the fire that he had once had in your life then it is time to step back and reevaluate why you fell in love with God and how to correct it.

His love for us is far deeper than we can ever imagine. Let us take a moment to reflect and meditate on God's love for our lives, *"In this the love of God was made manifest among us, that God sent his only Son into the world, so that we might live through him. In this is love, not that we have loved God but that he loved us and sent his Son to be the propitiation for our sins." 1 John 4:9-10* "Let us then with confidence draw near to the throne of grace, that we may receive mercy and find grace to help in time of need. *"*

Hebrews 4:16 *"So that you may be sons of your Father who is in heaven. For he makes his sun rise on the evil and on the good and sends rain on the just and on the unjust. "* Matthew 5:45 In John 17:25-26 it says, *"O righteous Father, even though the world does not know you, I know you, and these know that you have sent me. I made known to them your name, and I will continue to make it known, that the love with which you have loved me may be in them, and I in them. "* My notes to God may not be the same each day because each day is different, and it is not made to be the same. The beauty of each day is that God has a special note for us that he wants to show and read over to us. We must open and waiting for him to speak it to us. We must be receptive to what he is saying and speaking to us and the way he is speaking it. Sometimes God may use people to be a Conduent of the notes that he speaks to us or gives to us but neither of those people are able to capture the true heart of what God is saying unless he reveals it and says what needs to be said. The moment that we wait and hear God speaking to us and find his love notes in our lives we can then reach for more of his love notes in our lives through serving in church, helping out in the community, praying, going on missions trip, speaking life over those who are hurting and broken, and rescuing those that are going through. When we take a moment and pull back from our wants and desires and see and embrace the true heart of Jesus writing a love note then becomes a daily part of our lives.

We become accustomed to writing a note to God or singing to God or expressing our love to God. One of the things that I have learned is how to keep a heart that is centered solely on God. I press more into to God to keep my heart receptive to the things of God. I know that in doing so that I am preparing my heart to made new in God. In Psalm 51:10 it says that, "Create in me a clean heart, O God; and renew a right spirit within me." When our hearts are made new in Christ we are then permeated and receptive to the cleansing that it also includes. When we ask God to create in us a clean heart as David in the Bible was asking, we are pulling ourselves in absolute surrender to God. We are asking God to take away the heart has become decerped and foul before God and to replace it with a clean heart.

There is nothing more beautiful then something as great as our hearts becoming clean in God. We are showing to God that we are humble and that we are not in charge, but he is and that we place ourselves in complete surrender. That is what happens when we extend our invitation to God and ask him to give us a whole new heart. He is our creator and he has created our hearts in such a way that even our heart beats to him are distinctive. The almighty God our creator and redeemer understands the power behind our request for a new heart because he wants to restore every place in our lives and the heart is what beats the most for God and he will definitely create in us a clean heart so that our new notes that we now write to him will show our love in an even more profound way and his love notes to us will shape our lives in such a way that we are able to the power of his love in note that he gives us through the scripture of the word of God, through a song, through an angel, through a book, through a preacher, through a prophetic word, through our writings that we write to him and through our open and newly created hearts towards him. He speaks gently.

As I continue my journey in life my daily love notes become a daily part of my life and I press into him more and more each day and I look forward to leaving love notes to God. We must understand that even in the smallest of things that God has something great and powerful that he is going to do in us and through us. A love note takes only a second to do and it takes only a moment to write a small note to God and express our gratitude and appreciation to him for the things that he has done. It is amazing how one note can be so very powerful, but it truly is powerful, and it is a sign of love to God that is simple but extravagant to him at the same time.

It is amazing how one small note to God can be so breathtaking but when he leaves us love notes it is even more breathtaking because we are able to receive his love and hear him through the message of his word. I am excited about each time that God speaks to me and each time that I can receive the love that God gives to me in his love notes to me. When we are in a love relationship with God, he makes his love available to us even more because we are seekers of his love and we are taking the time that is needed to cultivate the relationship and to send notes of appreciation to him. A note can really change your life and a love note to God can make a difference in your life because you are able to share your love towards him through the expression of a love note. I look forward to writing more and more love notes to my daddy God.

Chapter Nine

Date Night with Daddy God

The most beautiful date that I have ever been on has been my date night with God. You may ask how anyone can date God? Or you may think in your mind that doesn't make sense. Well, the way that I spend my time with God and set aside time for God is my date night with him. It is a special time that I set aside, and I arrange my schedule in such a way that it fits accordingly to have a night out daddy God style. Don't get me wrong I have been on several dates before and had my share of enjoying expensive and even cheap meals but one of the greatest dinner dates in the one that I have turned my plate down and fasted and sought the face of God for my life because I wanted to see him glorified in my life. Our date night is one that is special candle lights, worship music and prayer.

I had to learn how to have a date night with God. When God started speaking to me about his love for my life in April of this year, I started to understand the value of why it was so important to my life. I learned why God has separated me in my life from so many things that I had been involved in that was not bring glory and honor to God. There is a great difference in knowing when something is right and doing what is right.

God spoke to me in 2018 that I needed to separate from the things that were going on in my life and that I needed to even step away from my marriage because it was not God-ordained. When he spoke those words to me, I immediately obeyed and followed them. I have been on a road to redemption and running for my life because the even has sought to destroy my life because of the word of God that abides on the inside of me and because of the calling on my life.

My love for God is not an infatuation but it is real and when I fell in love with God for real and surrendered my life to God for real that is when doors began to break loose in my that is when I saw the power of God begin to really move in my life when I exercised my faith and operated in obedience to God. When we learn to be fully obedient to God without asking him for something or questioning why he is doing what he is doing what he is doing. God's love for us is complete. When we take the time to spend time with God, he honors that time and he loves us for spending time with him and sacrificing by even having a date night with him.

I have even gone to lunch alone with God in mind but there is nothing as special like a date night where its myself and daddy God and we are enjoying the presence of one another without celebrating a special occasion but it is a just because moment because God honors our time with him more than we can ever imagine or think. I can't think about the good date night with God without first seeking the infallible love of the father. I can't think about how wonderful my date and time is with God without first seeing all the dates that I have been on in the past. When I focus on the wonderful and great cherished moments that I have it allows me to keep cherishing each date night that I get to have with God.

Going on a date night with God has also helped to bring healing in my life from past relationships with men that I have dated. Some of the relationships were sacred to my heart and I really loved deeply in them as much as I could but I was not able to fully embrace the heart of what love really was in my life because I had not yet fully experienced true love that had me head over my heels. I hadn't not found the one that I could not live without. For now, the only one that I could not bear to live without was God's love for me. I remember recently being on TV for God's Glory Radio Show and talking about love and the Father's love for my life. I spoke about how I would have date nights with God and how it was a special time for me because that was a shared time that I had made specifically for God and I to lay out everything that I was going through on the table and to really pour out my heart to him. For so long in my life I had been holding everything in and not speaking about it. I had been keeping my thoughts bottled up as if I were to continue in that pattern my thoughts would eventually explode, and I would have to pursue both counseling and get medical attention because of the severity of the nature behind it. For so many years I had built towards my relationship with God in a religious manner and not in a relational manner. When I became raw with God and began to start expressing my emotions and then learning how to manage my emotions I was then able to start building upon transparency in the past transparency with anyone absolutely scared me and I was not able to be as vulnerable in a relationship as I could have because a part of me was not all in with my love.

When I became all in with my love for God it has now helped me to become more transparent now that I have before and start thinking about and sharing my heart with others without a fear of what they would say or how they would react. I have lived most of my life not merely as free as I could have because of the fear of what others would think and say about me. I wasted so much time and energy worrying about things that I could not change and worrying about people that could care less about me. I can't bring back the time that was lost but I can allow God to heal heart and redeem the time for me. For all the years that were lost God has promised to restore them and to give me the promises that I had believed for such a long time.

The date night is my time to share the intimate things that God has placed on my heart to begin to unleash and unveil what those things are to him. There such a level of preparation that goes along with this in that when I have my special date night with God it is a time for me to really go all out and to enjoy it because I know that it is going to leave me with such a great reward of the presence of God just being there with me and having the bonding time that I need to keep going and to keep growing in my relationship with God. He is plummeting me forward in more things of him because it is truly my desire to grow deeper and to have that alone time with just me and God. This is the only time when it is okay for me to be selfish is when I have my date nights with God, and I dive in and press into the things of God more than I ever have before. The date night is a time for me to get raw with God and to bond with him with not being rushed. I spend so much time with people during the week, so I try to make my date night to be one that is on the weekend that is not busy.

It's a sacred time but it is also a fun time to just press into the presence of the Lord and to seek his face. I am not asking God for anything during the date night I am simply enjoying his presence and celebrating in the life that he has given to me. I have learned the power of appreciation in my date nights with God because it allows me to go into a new place in him in which I have never been and to seek more of his presence. The date night does not have to be long it can be an hour or three hours. It is whatever time that I have chosen it to be and it does not have a limit or a long drawn out schedule.

The moments that I get alone with God are sacred to me and I absolutely enjoy each moment because it creates a greater love for me towards God that continues to grow and operate within my life. It is in those alone times that I can become vulnerable to God and explain all my hurt, pain, disappointments, disagreements, happy moments, sad moments, dreams and my love and appreciation for God.

Chapter Ten

Communication never ends

Communication for me has always been a challenge. I am still working on becoming a better communicator every day. I closed myself down a lot in my relationships because I was not an effective communicator as I should be. It takes years to build communication that is solid and that has a strong foundation with others. Although I had a network on social media of friends with 5,000 on one site and 7,000 on another site, I still lacked the necessary components that were needed in my life to be an effective communicator. I had worked in customer service before and at call centers for years. I had experience speaking in the public and being around people but I lacked communication in so many avenues in my life and it ripped apart my relationship, my marriage, and it pushed people out of my life because I didn't know how to properly communicate.

I have had friends in my life that were experts at communication. They were counselors, educators, lawyers, doctors, and even writers. The important thing that I needed to learn how to connect with was in finding my voice. In finding my voice I was able to connect with my purpose and find what it was that I was trying to communicate and learn how to express myself effectively in order to do this it takes stepping back and taking myself out of the equation and then learning from God first and then from others on how to gravitate more to the divine protocol of my life that has been designed specifically for me.

I must learn the blueprint that has been dedicated to my DNA and then connect to it through onward communication. Effective communication takes time. Relationships are often destroyed due to lack of communication. Marriages end in destitution due to lack of communication. This was one area in my life that I had learn how to change so that I would not hurt myself and others in the process. My problem was deep inside of myself. I needed to seek God on how to become a better communicator not only for my sake but for the sake of others. When I found my voice, I was able to then become the voice that others needed. I learned that communication was not only for me but that it was in fact was for others that were connected to me. God designed as human beings to interact and connect with one another and to enjoy each other in conversation.

Sometimes social media takes away from that we end up with our noses in our phones instead engaging in real conversations. Real authentic conversations take vulnerability it takes expressing our pain, joy, and our lives with others. God wants that openness and that rawness from us, and he waits for it. He waits in anticipation to show us that he enjoys communicating with us and talking to us. He wants to be the audible voice that we reach out to in time of need even when we feel like he is not listening to us. He is in fact waiting and listening for us to call unto him.

The word of God says in Jeremiah 33:3, "Call to me and I will answer you and tell you great and unsearchable things you do not know." I love how it says unsearchable things because we don't always know what to communicate at the time, but God is waiting patiently and listening to our cries. In the unsearchable it means that we can try to give some of what is going on but God then takes it a little further and reaches more inward to what is actually going on and he looks for that in our conversations with him and in our communicating with him we gain a sense of peace in knowing that even if I can communicate some of what is going on in my life that its taking the first step and putting myself out there. This book and not easy for me. I have written several books before this one, but this book came as a challenge and it pushed me out of my comfort zone to write. That is what God wants us to do in our communication with him. He wants to push us out of our comfort zones and place us in position that keeps up moving forward in momentum.

Communication does that in our lives it keeps us moving towards what will happen next. In communicating we must learn how to step out of familiarity into the realm of deeper connectedness to God. Taking communication one stride as a time and working to gain momentum in the process helps to create a well-rounded conversation with God. The most ostentatious of it is that it's truly divine. Communicating with God is a remarkable and monumental thing to do. We learn how to express ourselves and welcome our lives into his path. God invites us on the most rewarding journey of our lives and that in conversations. Taking a moment to pause, express, speak, enjoy, and conversate even the more of topics and things that are disturbing us at the time.

There is no time limit in communicating with God because it is endless. Communication with God never ends it continues because there is so much at times that we have to say and get out and we can't place a time limit on that. We can embrace and look forward to more conversations and times to communicate with God. Communication does not have to end, and it will not end because there is more each day to speak on and talk on and to express to God. Communication grows over time and each time that I can express my true heart to God I can then make a greater difference in my communication patterns in my own life. Today I choose to communicate more and to love more.

I will not allow myself to be trapped in my emotions anymore. I will not allow myself to muzzle my own mouth and become afraid to speak out and to speak forth and to communicate on what is going on in my life and what is happening. I thought that I had to keep every part of my life private out of fear that people would turn on me and say things that they should not say about me. For so long I have been trapped in my own box of communication and I have allowed myself to succumb to a manner of living that was not helping my life hurting my life. When I learned how to open my mouth to God and to speak without fear it helped me to gain healing and deliverance in my life from the things that were trying to hold me hostage to my life.

In communicating with God there are no long arguments happening. It is simple a time for God and I to speak on what is happening in my life and to hear what I can do to help make the situation in my life better through his word. I have learned that in communication sometimes all that it takes is listening and hearing God's word to fully grasp what he is saying at the time. I don't ever want to rush the process of what God is doing in my life because I know that there is so much that he has to say to me at the time and I have to be ready and receptive to hear what God is speaking and saying to my life. As a prophetess of God that is one thing that I had to learn early on was ear training and learning to hear what God is saying first in order to speak and articulate it properly.

Going back and forth and never hearing what God says not only stops me from hearing what I need at the time, but it causes me to miss what is being said. I must learn that in listening in communication that there is no hurry to this that it is simply a moment, hour, or days at time that God is revealing something that he wants me to know. Communication with God never ends, and I had to realize that and acknowledge the profound beauty in this when I began to really reach deeper in my communication with God.

God is waiting to hear from us even when we think that he is not listening or that he has heard enough from us. The truth is that he loves to hear from us and to listen to what is going on and find out what he can do to make it better for us. When I pushed God away and didn't listen to him, I was missing out on help from God and what mattered the most for my life at the time. As a teacher now I have had to learn how to communicate and then overcommunicate in order to get the point across and to build

proper understanding and this is what God does for us.

Chapter Eleven

You loved me as you found me

One of my favorite songs by Hillsong is You loved me as you found me. In that song it has so much true meaning to my life in how God's love has found me right where I am, and it has rescued me from myself. I love to think of being found as being in the position of pain and distress that God came and rescued me right where I was, and he saved me from destruction. There have been times in my life where I have wanted to end my life because of the pain that I was going through. I thought that if it was ended there would be no more of the struggle that was going on but that was selfish thoughts from the enemy that was trying to destroy my life.

Being found where I am positions me to be at a stance of being in desperation and despair to a place of absolute surrender and grace. Being found takes time. Because the pursuer must observe, reflect, monitor, and strategize to find ways to meet the one that they are pursuing. That is what God does with us he waits. He listens. He observes. He strategically places at the right place at the right time so that he can meet us where we are which is at the place of being found. We can run, hide and think that we are escaping God's love for us only to find that we are running right into his arms of love. The place that no one dreams of being at often that place that is often our lowest. The place that we believe that God has left to die in. The place of being found positions us to be rescued by God's love.

Merriam Webster dictionary defines found as being the derivative of the word find. It means, "to establish (something) often with provision for future maintenance. The word find means that, "to come upon often accidentally, to come upon by searching or effort. That is what God does for us and that is what he did for me. He saw me at my lowest points in my which were in desperation of love and acceptance, broken, abused, homeless, abandoned, and lost. It was in the most dramatic time in my life that God found me. He found me way before I was worshipping on the pews at church. He found me long before I wanted to be found. For someone to find us they must first be searching for us and God has searched high and low to look for us even when it was convenient to just run away somewhere and to hide. The most powerful thing is that God still sees us and that we can never hide from him. Adam and Eve tried to hide from God after they had sinned. They were naked and ashamed. God covers us in our sins, and he wants us to know that even when are exposed to many things in our lives and we are ashamed that our shame can never push God away from us. It can only bring him closer to us.

God does not ask us if when we want to be found of him, he simply finds us and rescues us. We must get into such a place of surrender in our lives that we are in complete expectation for what God wants to do in our lives. We oftentimes block and hinder what God wants in our lives by being in a rush and doing things our own way instead of the way that God originally intended. God planned so much for us in the beginning of time in Genesis long before we walked the earth he had already planned and mapped out what our future was in life and there was nothing that we could ever do to take it away.

When we try to rush the process that God is doing in our lives, we have to then take a moment and slow down and hear what God is saying and what he wants us to do and not what someone is forcing us to do. God used the snake in the garden to entice Eve in the Bible with a forbidden fruit and she took the bait. How often do we buy into the lies of the enemy thinking that it will be okay and that we are going to okay if we sin when we are not? Sin leaves us high and dry there is no glory in it. In Genesis 2:25 it says that Adam and his wife were both naked, and they felt no shame." They had just entered the world and was not yet tainted to sin. God had given Adam the power to name animals and to give one of his ribs to his Eve his wife. In Genesis God dealt with Adam and Eve when they allowed the deception that they were hearing to come and speak to them. In Genesis 3:13 it said that, "Then the Lord said to the woman, what is this that you have done? The woman said, the serpent deceived me, and I ate. So, then Lord God said to the serpent, "Because you have done this, "Cursed are you above all livestock and all wild animals." God recognized the enemy and he rebuked and cursed the enemy. He also recognized and acknowledged the sin of both Adam and Eve. They were punished because of their sin but he allowed them to still live.

God must punish us when we have wronged not to hurt us intentionally but to show us that he loves us and wants to shield us from the dangers that this world brings to us. I was naïve to a lot of things in life because I was reared in a Christian home and there were expectations and rules that I had to abide by while living there and that is same in our Christian walk. God has given us The Ten Commandments to live accordingly to, he has given us his word to prepare and instruct us. He has corrected our lives with love in order that we may become made better in his image and to become more like he has desired us to live.

God desires that we live and walk in love daily. I had to learn how to view what loved looked like in the eyes of God. I had to see his love for my life really come alive in so many ways through my obedience to him. Not that we live as a slave to the sin in our lives that we have committed. Not that we live as a victim but as a victor. Not that we live in pain but in healing. Not that we live in deception but in truth. Not that we live in fear but in faith. Not that we live in jealousy but in celebration of others around us. Not that we live as peasants but as royal citizens of Heaven. Not that we live our lives out of order but that we live our lives in excellence.

Where are you finding yourself in this season? Maybe you too have faced being abandoned. Maybe you have faced betrayal in your life. Maybe you have faced misunderstanding. Whatever it is that you are facing you must come together and believe that God has not positioned you at this time to fail you. He has positioned you for healing, deliverance and promotion in this season. God had to show me that there is no perfect life and that I had to stop trying to be perfect and learn how to walk into the excellence that he wanted for my life.

God found me where I was in the valley of perfectionism. The scars of abuse from my past were immobilizing me. I had to understand what the difference between perfection and excellence was in order to move forward in embracing God's love for my life. In looking up the words excellence and perfection, I then learned that excellence it is the quality of being outstanding or extremely good whereas perfection is the condition, state, or quality of being free or as free as possible from all flaws or defects. God wants us to strive to be perfect but in that he is seeking that we live a life that is fulfilling towards him. In Matthew 5:8 it says, ""Therefore you are to be perfect, as your heavenly Father is perfect." In Psalm 19:7 it says that, "The law of the LORD is perfect, restoring the soul; The testimony of the LORD is sure, making wise the simple."

In Philippians 3:12 it says that, "Not that I have already obtained it or have already become perfect, but I press on so that I may lay hold of that for which also I was laid hold of by Christ Jesus." In 1 Peter 5:10 it says that, "After you have suffered for a little while, the God of all grace, who called you to His eternal glory in Christ, will Himself perfect, confirm, strengthen and establish you." God wants to establish our lives in his love and his promises for our lives. It doesn't have to take years to receive that perfect love from God. It can happen today in your life.

God wants us to come to him with open arms of love and surrender to his will. For me to embrace God's love for my life in totality I had to fall into God's open arms of love. I knew that it being in his arms of safety it would protect me from myself. Whenever someone hugs or embraces us it can sometimes be God hugging us them through them. God wants to hug and heal the pain and cleanse our lives for his glory. God's love is redeeming us from our past and healing us into our future in Christ. We cannot get there by embracing the baggage in our lives, but we get there by embracing the father's love for our lives in restoration and healing. I know for a fact that God is waiting for us with open arms because he loves us that much that he wants to see us in the fullness of the promise that he has for our lives.

The open arms from God are an extension to his love that is unfailing. Once we open ourselves in open surrender unto God, we can then experience the promise on an even greater level in our lives. God may find you in open arms and he may find you with closed arms. Be open and receptive to what God wants for your life in this season. You don't have to wait thirty years to get to newfound love that God has for you. You can embrace his love now for your life and experience the power of transformation that love makes in your life.

God is more than enough for me and he has helped me to realize that more than anything in this world that his love is the most important thing to my life right now. I celebrate the love that God has given to my life. I am not in a hurry anymore when it comes to love or even relationships. I am going to wait on God's best for my life and enjoy the times that I get to have with God. These are moments that cannot be replaced and I'm looking forward to receiving and enjoying the new moments with God's infinite love for my life in the arms of my father in Heaven.

Chapter Twelve

Intimate Moments with God

I have made a vow to myself that I am going to continue to fall in love each day with Jesus. It is at the intimate times in with life with him that I am stretched, empowered and liberated to live a life that extenuates life beyond reasoning in my faith. It dissipates doubts and replenishes it with faith. In my intimate moments with God it involves prayer, fasting, worship and dying to myself. For the first time in my life because I understand the divine nature of God's for me and how vital it is to my life, calling and purpose I can now step and embrace his love for my life. I no longer must run away from love or push love away because the love of Jesus has captured my heart in such a way that I am going to remain constant in him.

Each intimate moment that I can have with Jesus is special to my heart in that it's a sacrifice in my time that I don't mind sacrificing. I had to get to a place that I was so real with God and so real in my faith with God that I would not allow anyone or anything to shake my faith. I have learned to not take anything or anyone for granted anymore but to celebrate each breathing moment and each day with God.

There's so much that you must understand when you want to really grow in your relationship with God. It takes time. It takes patience. It takes love. It takes a sentence. And it takes you really wanting to grow for what you have gone through in your life is not always easy. And if we expect it to be easy, then we're looking for something that doesn't exist. And in God's love, is surely the existence that you need. Because His love, extends grace, extends peace and it extends patience

extends the love that we need for our lives. When I look at where I've come from, and where God has taken me, I understand that in the abuse, in the hurt, in the eating disorders, In the misunderstanding, in the abandonment, In the search for answers to love, that I was then able to gravitate to the real love of Christ my life. It wasn't in love of man or the love in others, or the love in what I could thought I could extinguish myself. But it was solely in the love of God, that I found his love for me. And maybe you're at that place right now. Yet you're standing in, and you don't recognize that God loves you. And that there are no strings attached, that there is simply love only for you.

You must know that you are loved. You must know that there is so much power in the love that God has for you. You must know that his love is so deeply for you that it can never be changed. It can never be disrupted, it can never be erased, because it's that powerful. The same God that fought for my love is the same God that will fight for you. The same God that helped me to recover from shame is the same God that will help you to recover from what you're going through. The same God that helped and healed me to a mask every area of my life that I was feeling that I had to cover and keep hidden in my life is the same God that will build those pieces inside of you and bring you to the complete deliverance that you need for your life. Stop hiding and start a Brit embracing what God has for you.

I know I have reiterated and expressed this a lot throughout this but there is, so beauty founds in God's grace for our lives we allow God to heal your wounds instead of yourself. When you allow God to heal those broken areas and not run away from them. You ever just wanted to feel loved? Have you ever just wanted to experience love? Have you ever just wanted to fall in love again? It can happen. Because in God's love is endless. In God's love. He wants to give you those intimate moments with him. And God's love. He wants to shower you and position you for the promise for your life And God's love. He wants to take you deeper with a purpose in mind, and God's love. He wants to show that you can go all in for His glory. In God's law is where the promise for your life extends. You must learn to break free into the promise to love. You must learn that there is so much power and expectancy of the love of God for your life, that you are now reckoning to flow even more in his love. Because in the everlasting promise that he has for your life, you can then grow and gravitate to that love by being all that he wants you to be and more.

It's time for me to stretch. It's time for me to grow in my love for the Lord. It's time for me to become intimate more with him. And to understand the intimate moments of promise that are available for my life. It's time for me to really dive in and stop waiting on something and go after what he has my life. It's time for me really to go into the intimate secret closet places the promises that the Lord has for my life, and really searched to develop and growth as a woman of God that He has called me to be during the season. There's no more time to waste. There's no more time to wait. There's no more time to linger and under Try to understand what the problem is. But to really focus on what God has called me to do.

I can't focus on what does not exist in my life. I cannot focus on what I wish I could have had and what I could have done better. But The thing that I have to hold on to is the promise of God's love in my life, the promise of hit the intimacy that I will now embrace in my life, The promise of the joy and celebration of knowing that all that happened before does not have to be a part of my life any longer. And it's now a time for me to go deeper in the promises of what God has in my mind and in my emotions and in my purpose. I'm now all in for Jesus. There's no turning back. There is no looking back. There's no stepping back. I am all in because he is all in for me and I'm going to give all my love for him. It is a cherish time of diving in pressing forward that I understand the promises now that God has in my life and move past the point of trying out why I did not understand them before.

Take my love even farther. I had to understand that there was a point that I needed to go deeper, deeper and my relationship with God, deeper in my thought patterns, deeper in my, knowing that there was more to what God had for my life. In order to understand what going deeper meant. At first have had to look into the definition of deep and understand the power of what it means to go deeper, and in finding that I understood then that deep meant to extend far down from the top, or surface, very intense, or extreme. And then to follow on to that I understood, even further that going deep meant extending far from some surface or area such as an extending far downward, a deep well, a deep chasm extending well inward from an outer surface, a deep gash or deep says the animal. When I investigate the word deep and makes me further in my thoughts of knowing that there's something far greater, that is inside of me.

When I look at the word deeper it also helps me to understand that in the intensity of the deep, that is there, there's always the after effect of what comes from going beyond. And what I mean by that is that in the beyond is the furnace of going more inside of the surface area of our life, we must search for what

137

is deeper inside of us. We must look for those broken places we have to look for the broken parts that needs to be fixed and we must work on fixing them. Because if we don't, we lose out on healing, we lose out on relationships, we lose out on love. Now, that's not to say that God is not going to continue to love us, that is not something that will happen because God will continue to love you. But the more that you begin to love yourself and you're able to love others, you can step out of the box of where you are, and your deep pattern thoughts of what love should be or what love should look like or how love exists, it's so long for you that you're able to really evolve and feel the effectiveness of what is involved in love. And what I mean by that is you must go deeper and find out what that is.

You have to search for what the purpose is for that deepness you have to look beyond the level of what that love was before, and see what that love has now become when I did this, I was able to understand that going deeper and my relationship with God was important. It was not something that I regretted or didn't feel that I need it but it's something that I wanted for my life because I wanted to experience God's love just that great. I wanted to experience His love, beyond the surface area. I wanted to experience His love, in a way that I had never experienced before. And the only way to do that was to get raw with myself to look at myself in the mirror and say how much do I want to be loved. How much do I want to be accepted? How much do I want to be changed? How much do I want to go deep deeply in my walk with the Lord.

And that is not always easy for me. It's not always easy for anyone. And if it is easy for you then that's a wonderful thing. But when you must really stretch yourself and go beyond what you're used to, and start really pushing into what felt good before, and then move past that and then go into what feels even better now. That's a stretch, because anytime that you stretch yourself, you are pulling the last city of what you experienced beforehand, into a deeper gratitude of what you're experiencing now, because it pulls you in allows you to be stretched. It's kind of like that of a rubber band, being stretched because you must end the rubber band stretching the material as to the pic on itself to be even stretched forward. So that is what God has done for me in this season. He has allowed me to be stretched like that rubber band, he's allowed me to not pop, to not snap to not lose it, and the process of all that I've gone through, because it can be so impactful that you know you can lose your mind in the process of the things that you're going through, but God holds their mind together. He holds you together because he loves you just that much. He wants to see you, developed, he wants to see you process and grow and to all that He has for you, like, you cannot get to where you supposed to be by holding on to what was what could have been the way that you go deeper is by going beyond the surface level of where you are and propelling yourself into what you need to be in.

And when we go to a deeper level and God, we're able to experience that because then our purpose becomes not just on the outer level, but it becomes even more deeper, to what God has called us into the reason why you are reading this book today may not be the reason why someone else is reading it. The reason that someone else picked this book up men may have been the cover may have been the title may have been because they had been through pain in their life maybe they have experienced a pattern and a lot that they don't understand why they went through, but for whatever reason you are reading this I'm thankful for it, but God wants to thank you even more because he wants to let you know

that is not by accident that you have picked up this book today is

not by accident that you have gone beyond the pages, and to this

chapter that you're in. Now the last chapter of this book that he has

begun to even revelation to you why you are reading this book,

God has a purpose for you, and his purpose. He wants you to know

and understand that there is a deeper, call to your life, there is a

deeper level of love that you are reaching your life, there is a

deeper promise that God will extend to your life, but you have to

be willing to step out of the area that you're in now, and embrace

what he is taking you. There was so much stretching that has

happened in my life, even down to the level of how I am eating in

my life now God even shifted me to becoming a vegan. Now that

to me was a complete stretch because I had been used to eating

chicken. I've been used to eating fried foods I've been used to

eating French fries and pizza. So that was a complete stretch from

my life, but in the shifting of the eating pattern that God has me on

to be a vegan. I've developed even more better than my health, my

cholesterol has decrease, and I feel a lot better physically and I

look a lot younger physically, because of the God, God being obedient to God and allowing him to tell me what to eat during that time and how to save my health, and how to save my life. So, all of the things that I've gone through in my life have not been by accident, even in the area of the birth functioning of my life you know even the birth order of being the middle child, God knew that there are some things that I need to push my sister into, and to push my brother into, and the only way that he can allow me to do that he was strategic in the planning of the process of where he positioned me, and where he placed me, and where he put me so that I would know that there was more to what he had in store.

And God is really pushing me even further now to let me know that if I'm going to be all in for him, or I'm going to be all out for him because I need to know and develop inside of myself that I am going to be all out for the Lord. I'm going to go live my life sold out for him so deeply that it doesn't matter anymore, what people say or what people think or what they're expressing towards me, because I have to know that the love that God has inside of me is far greater than what anyone can say or do or try to harm me or do to me in the process.

And I had to break free from the opinions of others, you know, in doing that it's an it's a process because we feel that we must appease people we have to please them. So God is showing me during this time that I don't have to please people anymore, that I don't have to live my life, up to the standards of man, but the only standards that I had to live up to is the standards of God, His love for my life has loved me to the point of knowing that that I had to break free into His presence into his love and to his grace and to his companionship from my life and not my own.

So, there has come an expectancy with that. There's come the expectancy of knowing God's love for my life there's come to expect to see a knowing that I am Furthermore and looking forward to being loved daily. I'm looking forward to being love even more because of God because of his love for my life and that is how we must live our lives in the expectancy of His love. The expectancy of His grace. The expectancy of what He has promised to us. And I know that in the everlasting grace of God's love for me, that there's so much more, because when I look at the word everlasting, that to me represents so much more than my finite mind could ever think because when you think of the word everlasting, that in itself is powerful. That means lasting forever for a long time.

So, the, knowing that God's love for me is everlasting, that in itself is powerful, because that means that it's going to go from now to eternity, that there's no ending to it, that there's nothing that I can do to end that because His love is for me. So that is the everlasting promise that God has for our lives is the everlasting grace of his love for us. And when we have that great love in our lives, we're able to experience the power of what he has brought us to where he has birthed us into. And now it's not always an easy process of knowing that but it has taken me in my 30s now to experience that and I'm grateful for this because God's love is just so beautiful to me, and I'm able to experience His love and the magnitude now that I've never been able to experience before because I've opened myself up to, to be loved and to receive love and to go further in the love of God.

And because of this love, I've been know that there is a Promise of Hope beyond this, that I'm looking to be in the everlasting love that He has for my life and I'm hoping that that is the same that you're wanting for your life is to experience the everlasting love that He has for you. Be everlasting love that He has given to you the everlasting love that he wants to pour you the everlasting love that he wants to shower on you today. Be everlasting love that he wants to extend to you today. You must know in yourself, that there is so much more to where your life has been and where you're going and where you want to go when you want God to take you.

This is my story and my story are not the same as yours is not meant to be the same as anyone else's because your story is not always designed to be with someone else's story is. And so in that you must know that there's purpose, there's love, and there's grace and there's everlasting love for your life, you have to look to receive that you have to look to understand that you have to look to believe that and know that, and gravitate to that promise of what God has for your life, and really knowing that, in his promise, there's so much grace towards you, and there's so much that he wants to do in the process of it all.

So, take thought on this today and really sit back and ponder on the love of God for your life. The love of God for your life. Not anyone else's life, but for your life. And really come to understand and know that there's power and love that there's grace in love, that there's truth and love that there's healing and love, and that God's love for you is just that valuable that when you learn to really grow in love and find completion and love. You will then receive the full love of God in your life.

I want to share with you about how important the everlasting love of the Father is for your life.

And the way to do that is to web typically show you from the Bible, on how it is important to your life. The Book of Psalm 36:7 that how precious is your unfailing love Oh God, how precious is your unfailing love, oh God.

And then in Psalm 86:15 It says but you O Lord our God, merciful and graces slow to anger and abounding and steadfast love and faithfulness. Give thanks to the God of heaven. For his steadfast love endures forever Psalm 136:26, the Lord your God is in the midst, a mighty one who will say, he will rejoice over you with gladness, he will be quiet. with you by his love, he will exalt over you with loud singing Zephaniah three and seven. You must

understand that nothing can change God's love for you. In john

3:16 it says, For God so loved the world that He gave His only

Son, that whoever believes in Him should not perish but have

everlasting life.

In john 15:19-17. It says, as the love, the Father has loved

me so have I loved you abide in my love. If you keep my

commandments, you will abide in my love. Just as I have kept the

Father's commandments and a bottle of His love. These things

have I spoken to you that my joy may be in you that your joy may

be full. This is my commandment that you love one another as I

have loved you. Greater love has no man than this that the

someone laid down his life for his friends. You are my friends.

If you do what I command you no longer do I call you

servants, for the servant does not know what his master is doing

for I've called you friends for all that I have heard from my father

I've known to you. You did not choose me but I chose you, and

appointed you that you should go and bear fruit, and the fruit

should abide so that whatever you ask the Father in my name, he

may give it to you. These things I command you that you will love one another in john 15:19-17 And first Corinthians 13:4-8 it says, Love is patient, love is kind, it does not envy, it does not boast. It is not proud. It always protects always trusts, always hopes always perseveres.

Another powerful scripture about God's love is that, Romans five and eight says God's God show his love for us, and that while we were sinners Christ died for us.

Then one of my other favorite scriptures that I love is glaciers two and 20 and it says I had been crucified with Christ. It is no longer I who live, but Christ who lives in me the life I now live in the flesh I live by the faith in the Son of God who loved me and gave himself for me.

Isn't that powerful God's love. Because in his love. There is no failure in his love. There is peace. There is kindness there is happiness, and there is joy in john three and was it says see what kind of love the Father has given to us that we should be called children of God. So, we are the reason why the world is a note us is that I did not know him. In john first john four seven through eight, it says, beloved. Let us love one another. For Love is from

God. Whoever loves has been born of God and knows God,

anyone who does not love does not know God, because God is

love.

Each day I want to make it my business to completely

know God and to completely understand the revelation of what

comes from love, and the revelation of what comes in side of love

in doing that I know that the ultimate sacrifice is not persist with

me, but that it persists with others as well that love is a two way

street you have to give love and you have to receive love, so I'm

finding now that my love of God is continuing to grow even more

because I've decided to step outside of myself and really strongly

fall in love again with God, and really grow in my relationship

with him. I know that it is important to find that love and peace in

God by sacrificing by developing a more stronger relationship with

the Lord, and not simply settling for less, but going deeper in

seeking more of his presence, seeking more of his love, seeking

more of his promises for me.

This book for me has brought healing to my life. For

many of you it will do the same, because you need to experience

the power of God's love for real. You may have experienced love, this is your time in your life where you actually experience the power of God for real in your life when you come to the full understanding of what God's love truly means for your life, and why it is so important at this stage in your life to actually receive it, because in his promise. There is grace, there is love and there's assurance of knowing that his promise for you is so important.

There may be times in your life where you feel like you don't deserve love, and I've been there too I've been at the place in my life where I felt for so long. That was what I was experiencing I was not embracing the love of God of my life. And because of that, it hindered me in really receiving the promises of what he had for my life because I wasn't really able to gravitate fully to what he had in store for me because I was so used to what I wanted and what I wanted to do.

So, I had to really stretch past that and develop a mindset of, there is more, but I must search for it. There is more, but I have to go deeper and find it there is more but it's not going to take me sitting around waiting for it to happen for it to happen that I actually have to physically find it and physically search for it, and physically dive deeper and to what he is wanting, and to experience His love. I've come to know that I can experience that in the spirit as well that His love is just so amazing to my life.

And some of you may have picked up this book thinking it was, you know, just another love story, or it was just something that was just talking about God's love. But this is far greater than that love. This is not just any love story this is a story of the amazing turnaround of how God changed my life for the better and calls his love to heal me and deliver me in the process. It's a story of how God, pick me up and my place of brokenness and healed me and rescued me of myself so that he can really go deeper inside of where I had improperly trained me to be all that I am today. I had to really step aside, of what I had known before. And really embrace what I am knowing now and finding that true love in Christ. I am going to always know that he loves me. Because he does love me.

God's love is forever. It is constant in this forever. And I must understand his love in my life. Jesus went to the cross to bear the ultimate sacrifice of love for our lives. How great is that. His love, His promise. His sacrifice, so that we could be free of sin.

That to me is powerful. Because I'm no longer a slave to sin, but I'm now walking in the freedom of which Christ has given me and his love for my life today God is going to pour his love on you. As you're finishing up the last pages of his book, he's pouring his love on you even now.

May you experience the power of God's great love for your life.

May you never be the same because of the love that is on these pages from God. That will fill your life forever. May be filled with the promises of His love and experience the power of His greatness and knowing that God's love this healing you and making you anew. And it's making you complete in him that his love is restoring every area of your life. His love is unleashing a breaking point that you've never experienced before. The power of His great love is coming in you even now. The you're feeling the promises of what he is doing for you. Not what man is doing for you, but what God is doing for you.

The you are now coming to embrace all that He has for your life and more, because he desires to take you to a deeper place. Don't you want to go deeper. Once you tired of being in that same place that you were in years ago. It's time to go deeper. It's time to stretch further. It's time to look past all the pain of the past, and really stretch forward into the future promises of what God has for your life. And coming to love those come to love Jesus. He is for everything. He is for love. He is your peace. He is your promise. He is your strength. He is your grace. He is your wisdom.

His love for you is everything. Are you willing to follow the love of God, again, and get back to that place where you were before? It's time. It's time to get back to that place in God, and maybe you don't even know who God is. and I will love to share with you on how to do that

is called accepting Jesus Christ into your heart in loving him. I did this year ago, and now my life has forever change. He has brought forgiveness into my life. He's healed me from eating disorders. He's healed me from abuse. He's helped me to get over the pain of my past. He's helped me to get over and to be delivered from perfectionism and embrace excellence.

He's helped me to live a life beyond where I've could have ever imagined. Because of the grace and love that he had for my life. Not that anything that I had ever done. But it was all the love from him. The love of my Father, Jesus Christ. He loves you so much. He wants to embrace you today. He wants to show you how important you are to him. He's not going to force himself on you, because he's not that kind of a God. He loves you so much that he'll meet you right where you are. You don't have to have a fancy tie or fancy suit, because he just loves you. That is what I had to come to understand.

God loves me, right where I am in that his everlasting love this fighting daily for me. In his fighting for me. He delivered me. He saved me. It gave his life for me, so that I may live again. And I'm excited, because one day I'll be rejoicing in heaven with my brothers and sisters in Christ, singing the songs of the angels and rejoicing for others that are to come and celebrate the goodness of the grace of my God. Are you ready? Are you ready to embrace the love of God? Are you ready to embrace his full love for your life? Then truly fall in love with him today. Makes a day to day that your life changes forever, and really fall in love of God. And always know that I love you. And it's not by accident that you picked up this book today. But know that there's a greater love and the promise of which God has given you. He wants you to know that you are forever love, and that his forever love is going to change you. And that his forever love is waiting for you in his

forever love is going to bring transformation into her life that you

will come to know and to experience. Unknown

Well we anticipate love. It creates a greater facet of where love

comes from. Because we are in the place of receiving and

anticipating it to happen.

So, in order to experience that we first must anticipate it.

So, what anticipation means then is the action of anticipating

something expectation, or prediction anticipation also is an

emotion involved in pleasure, excitement, or anxiety or awaiting

something to happen.

So that is what God is going to have happened to you in this season

is that you're going to experience His love, in a way that you have

never experienced before. But you first must anticipate that it's

going to happen. You must be ready and anticipation of what must

happen and what is to come.

And that is what God's love does for us, it creates a

feeling of anticipation, where we're waiting for more because it's

just that wonderful it's just that great, it's just that expected of what

we are wanting in our lives. And the more that we anticipate the love of our father, the more that we continue to grow in his love and develop in his love and experience the power of His love. I believe that many of us are not where we should be in God, in finding the love that we need for our lives in experiencing more of us love is because we have adapted to the mindset of that we don't need his love. And when we do that, we are not in absolute surrender of what God has for our lives, when we fail to anticipate more what he can do for us. And when we know how important that is and we develop an understanding of how important that is it can then push us and into the true promise of what he has for our lives. In, I am at that place of anticipation in my life because I want more of the Lord in my life, and I want to see my life change I want to see things happen. I want to see the place that I was in, years ago be one as a testimony to many of the goodness of the Lord and I want to see this book, come as a testimony to the lives of people.

And just from stepping out of my comfort zone and telling people you know you can be healed and delivered from an eating disorder, you can be healed and delivered from perfectionism you can be healed and delivered from abuse, you can be healed and delivered from the fear of man and you don't have to have approval of this addictions anymore. You don't have to want to be accepted so badly that you do things that you normally would never have done in your life, and I've been there at the point of wanting to be accepted. So equally by others that I put off what I know to do is right in order to please, another, and you never want to position your place yourself in a place of that, and that you lower your standards of your walk of God to please another because, you know, what is truth in the Bible, so you shall know the truth and the truth shall make you free.

And in that freedom comes holiness in that freedom comes a mindset of wanting to live an order of what God is saved, and what His Word says concerning our lives. And in that promise is also the acknowledgement of anticipation, but also the acknowledgement of knowing that his word stands. And what I mean by that is the word of God, stands forever. We may try to alter it or put it in the place of how we want it to go or depicted in any way that we should, but the Word of God is for real is the word of God says it's alive and active piercing even the dividing asunder is you know the word of God is just that powerful. When we have to know that in the power of the word is the true transformation of where I live changes when you are at the place in your life where you are positioning yourself to fully look in the mirror and see the person on the other side and want to change that person, that becomes real because you are wanting to experience the fulfillment of the promise of what God has for your life because you're no longer waiting on receiving love, but you have come to understand that love changes that love heals that love transforms that love sets free, and in that love that you're expecting from the Father He wants to give you that love today. He wants to birth, a new a new beauty of his love for her life the love of holiness, the love of truth, the love of his word, the love of his character, the love of doing what he has called you to do for such a time as this.

It is not in chasing dreams that we thought we could have had instead of going after the dream of what God has for our life.

Don't get me wrong I'm not against anything as far as ambition or dreams. What I'm saying is sometimes we put off what God is telling us to do, and we end up going around years and years meander Lee, doing things that we should not do. Because of what we felt that we should do in our heart was what we wanted and not what God wanted. So, I want to save a lot of you time and energy into putting your action into something that does not profit your life at all, and put your life in the place of position of going after what he has truly promised for your life. I believe when we get to that place of understanding what purpose is that we can then reach further in our anticipation of what he has in store for us.

So, I had to first understand why my purpose was just that vital and why the purpose that he had for my life was just that important. And one of the things that the Lord had revealed to me, concerning my purpose was he did let me know that I was chosen. And when you chose and you're just you stand out, there's a highlighter, showing you like yours, yours, you're going to stand out no matter what, when you've been chosen. So, in that he helped me to understand what my purpose means, and the meaning of my purpose is the meaning of my call. But before that, to understand the definition of what purpose is for your life first and then understand what your purpose is, is essentially important of knowing where you're going. So, purpose means the reason for which something is done, or created in which something exists.

Have as once intention or objective intention is a mental state that represent a commitment to carry out an action or actions in the future, intention involves mental activity such as planning or forethought. When you have purpose in your life, you're able to make life decisions that are vital to your wellbeing, you're able to have a behavior, you're able to set goals for yourself, understand the connectedness of where you're going and satisfying your responsibilities of your calling in life, and my calling in life is to be a preacher as well as a teacher, and to present the gospel of Jesus Christ to the world and to also teach. So that's my purpose but also to do missionary work and to also write books.

And so, God has given me this as a gift to get the word out to others to share to people. And I don't take that lightly because it's an important thing to me that I share and carry the Word of God effectively, because I don't want to do anything to this heart. The what God has called me to do during this time of my life, so I want to make sure that what I'm doing has purpose. What I'm doing has a complete understanding in what I'm doing is effective. So, and the effectiveness of this, I want my purpose then to be so effective and life changes that people understand from reading my books that why their purpose is just that important.

And the purpose of love is first to anticipate the love and then

afterwards to, to find the understanding of it, and to embrace it.

So, God's love for you is important you must anticipate

his love. You must understand the purpose behind his love, you

must grow to accept the love that he gives for your life and

embrace it fully. Because God has so much love that he wants to

pour into you, and he wants to change your life and bring great

purpose to your life. And when you're able to understand why

you're here, why you exist, why your life happened, why your

story happened, the testimony behind your life, and why things

have come as they are. You didn't realize that it was not by

happenstance but that there was a purpose behind it. That was

clearly involved in what he wanted for your life, potentially, and,

you know, it may take years. It may take months or may take days

and for some it may take weeks, but whatever your point is that

you're finding your love relationship with God, coming to its next

level and coming back to the place where it needs to be. That's

important. And when you reach for more of his love. When you

reach for more of his grace when you reach for more of him in the season. He will reveal Himself into you in a way that you've never imagined before because its purpose is then found greater. His purpose is developed through its purpose is relinquish through you.

And so now you're able to really flourish in all that He has for your life because of the promises of him. That is important. We must realize that and know that. Because when we do, we can reach for it into all the things that he has for us. What is your purpose today? Do you want to experience purpose and love? Are you ready to anticipate God's great love for you? Are you ready to embrace the promises that He has for your life? Are you anticipating more of his love than you ever have before? Are you struggling to meet his love, where he needs you? Or are you just waiting. What are you waiting on today? May your anticipation not be one that fails, but maybe one that reaches the promise that you've always wanted in God, in which is his love for you. His love for others and his love for those around you, and his love for those that are connected to you. His love for that he has promised for you for so long, is now being poured out to you today for so long. I have learned, God's love.

And now I'm able to really embrace what that love is and enjoy it. And it's helped me now to have better relationships with people and to really understand who I am and to walk in that promise. Forgiveness in my life. Because in love, you must forgive. You must forgive yourself first and then forgive the other person and move on and enjoy what he has for you. In in doing that. It takes time, because you may not always want to forgive, and you may not always want to move on. But when you do it changes your life for the best so forgiving yourself is important and it's just as important as forgiving the other person. So, in forgiveness. Forgiveness means that it's an intentional involuntary process by which a victim undergoes a change of feelings, and attitudes regarding an offense, and let's go of those negative emotions and venture illness, and it's an actual process of being forgiven and forgiving.

So, when you forgive, just as God has forgiven you. What greater promise is love than that? God's love is just that wonderful inefficiency says in Ephesians 4:32, it says Be kind, one to another, tender hearted forgiving one another, even as God for Christ's sake has forgiven you. God's love wants to forgive you and has already forgiven you. Are you ready to forgive yourself? Are you ready to anticipate love?

Are you ready to experience how his love will forever change you to the place of where you will never go back to where you were before? Are you ready to anticipate the promises of God for your life? Are you ready for the anticipation of love? Are you ready to anticipate his great love for you? It's available. Just open your heart. Just open your spirit, and be receptive, of what he has for you. Me Your journey of love, the one that is finalize what the love of God always staying strong, knowing that in receiving his love. You will be forever changed.

You don't always have to stop the past. But what you can accept is the future. The future of the promise that God has for your life. God's word says that he has a future for you. And this word he promises us a hope and unexpected, and in that, we find that we come to accept the Lord at a greater capacity than we've ever imagined.

It is through God's love that you're able to experience the true freedom as a believer in the walk as a Christian that he has called you to be. He must understand that from the beginning of time until now, that God has always wanted you to accept his love for your life, to not feel guilty about accepting God's love. Do not feel afraid to accept His love, do not feel like you are not worthy of His love, because you are worthy, and you are loved. You are celebrated by God the Father. He wants to celebrate you today, and he wants you to accept Him into your heart into receive His love, that He has given for you.

      I had to learn that my past was simply that my past. And that God will use it as a story and as a testimony to change the lives of others. But I'm not to dwell on that and to live in that experience again or to go back to it and try to relive it. But what I am to do is accept the love that God's given me in the process, and accept the love and he's given me so graciously so that I may walk and go into the place that he's called me to go into.

      You don't know what's waiting for you on the other side of the door, unless you will step what you have. So that is what God has done in my life during this time is he's pushed me to really start writing again, and to really push myself even more and to go into a greater momentum of what he has my life because in this accelerated season of my life there is so much more that he wants to do. And I cannot allow fear or anything to discourage me from the process of what he has my life. And that, in that I have to accept, I have to believe, and I have to know and I have to have the faith and accepting that his love for me is just that wonderful his love music that great, and I have to speak boldly with myself and know the in the confidence that He has for me that is so much greater. And I must know that I can't keep waiting for something to happen that I must know that is going to happen. So, when I stepped as love, I'm able to embrace it. When I steps is love, I'm able to gravitate to what he has. When I accept his love, I'm able to step out of my comfort zone and really into what he has for my life. And then that part I'm able to really define, who I am and to really develop myself to be all that he has called me to be. I learned to accept God's love. How beautiful are the feet of those who preach the gospel of Jesus Christ?

So, I am thankful that God not only blesses me at a level that I'm able to bless others, and loves me at a point to where I'm able to love others, but at the same time I'm able to grieve onto others and love that they truly need, and extend that love, such a way that it transforms and changes their lives for the better. That is

what I'm looking for God's into my life. I'm looking for him to

continuously. Allow me to be changed through his love, and I'm

always going to accept and enjoy the love that he has my life

because he has been my healed.

He has been my deliverer, he's been my friend and he's

been my father, and he's been my assurance of knowing that I don't

have to stay in this place that I'm in right now, but there is a greater

promise beyond this place, and that promise says that in accepting

his love that there is greater, and accepting his love there is more

and accepting his love, there is a greater promise beyond what I

have been expecting, and I can reach towards that. And I can really

gravitate to what he's saying.

Because I want that for my life, I want to see the Lord.

Move in my life I want to see my life transform, and I want to see

greater things happening in my life because of where I am right

now. And that may be what you're looking for you. Maybe you're

looking for that change. All you have to do is accept the love of

God, and a step where he has realized that he wants to bring that

change to your life, and all you have to do is be willing to step, take that next step and the step his love and know that his love is the greatest love for your life. I hope that you're able to fall in love with Jesus, as I have, because it's been the greatest thing that has ever happened to me and my life will never be the same because I've known the power of falling in love with Jesus. Are you ready to experience the power of his love for your life and embrace his love being poured out on you?

I had to make the decision that I was no longer gone to stay in my comfort zone and that I was going to receive all of God's love that was intended for my life and more. It's time to raise the standard in our lives and in the lives of our families and begin a new reassured love walk with Christ that is monumental to our lives. It's not time to chase after lust but it's time to chase to the true love of God and his divine nature and love for our lives as the Bible has intended for our lives.

Today I choose to accept God's love for my love over everything in this world. Receiving his love will empower me and help to eradicate and bring love and change to the lives of others. I was once that little girl that was afraid and abandoned. I was once that teenager struggling with an eating disorder and trying to fit in.

I was once that adolescent trying to be perfect and gain approval and acceptance from others. I have now become the woman that does not fear man any no longer and I love and embrace the God in me and the God over me. I have been changed by the power of love of Christ and I am made new because of God's resurrected love in my life.

A Special Prayer for you

Father, in the name of Jesus, I pray for every person that has read this book today me this chapters on these pages forever change their lives. May they come to know the promises that you have for their lives father, maybe know that your ultimate love is sacrifice of how you went on the cross was to change their lives forever, and that you have the greatest gift of all, which is love for their lives. I ask you, Lord that you will bless each reader that you've changed their lives Lord God, that they will never be the same that healing and deliverance will take place in our lives, and that you will bring so much deliverance to them and their families. And Lord, I thank you that you will change them so much so that they will go out and bring healing deliverance to others from what you have done in their lives. Lord, I pray that this book will be a conduit of your love, and I can do one of your grace for their life and that reading through these pages will not just be another story to them, but it will be one that will bring healing and deliverance to every person that reads this book today. And Lord, I ask you to bless and heal each person will God bring out every issue in their lives and bring forgiveness and healing into the lives of every person Lord, may

they come to know and understand the great power of your love. In

Jesus name, amen.

ABOUT THE AUTHOR

Dr. Monique Rodgers formally known as, Dr. Monique Vann is an author, Global speaker, Prophetess, ordained minister, educator, entrepreneur and woman on the mission for God. Dr. Monique Rodgers completed her undergraduate at Oral Roberts University in Tulsa Oklahoma being a first-generation college student she didn't stop there she went on to obtain her Master of Science degree from Colorado Technical University where she maintained a 3.97 GPA. She then loved education so much that she went on to pursue her doctorate degree at Colorado Technical University in Global Leadership. She has traveled to five nations: Africa, Mexico, Peru, Jamaica, and Thailand.

She is currently an English as a Second Language Teacher online at Education First. She is also a 7th grade mathematics teacher at PreEminent Charter School. Dr. Rodgers also serves as an International Advisory Board Member for Daddy's Provision for his Daughters International, Inc. She is an International Distinguished Scholar. She is the founder of Repairing the World Through the Word Ministries in Raleigh North Carolina. Dr. Monique Rodgers has been a guest on radio programs such Rashael Speaks. She has a weekly broadcast called the Power Lunch Broadcast on The Glory Network. Dr. Rodgers has also spoken on tv at God's Glory Radio TV Show. Dr. Rodgers always knew that God had called and gifted her to preach and to write.

When she was seven years old, she hand wrote books and sold them for quarter to her friends. She always knew that she was destined to be a scribe and a writer for God's glory. Her writing has been truly that a gift comes easier for her than most to complete. She has self-published five books. Her first book was a collection of poems called Poems of Inspiration. Her next book was called Hello! My name is Millennial, following that she wrote,

A More Simple Life, A Majestical Land of Twinville, Picking up the Pieces and she is now looking forward to completing her newest book in the Write with Me Writers Challenge called, Falling in Love with Jesus. After the challenge she has also decided to write another book called Accelerate. Dr. Rodgers is also a vegan and advocates when she can for heath events. Her passion is for helping the lost, hurt and the broken for Jesus. She has studied at the Black Business School and preparing to work on her certification in Business Analytics at Harvard Business School online. She has also completed her associate degree in Biblical studies and Theology at International Miracle Institute in Pensacola, Florida. She aspires to leave a legacy to her family. Dr. Rodgers is a survivor she has overcame abuse, eating disorders, and homelessness.

Made in the USA
Columbia, SC
27 November 2019